Junior Skill Builders

BASIC MATH
in
15 Minutes a Day

Junior Skill Builders

BASIC MATH in 1.5 Minutes a Day

LEARNINGEXPRESS®

NEW YORK

S

Published in the United States by LearningExpress, LLC, New York.

Library of Congress Cataloging-in-Publication Data:
Junior skill builders : basic math in 15 minutes a day.
    p. cm.
  ISBN: 978-1-57685-660-4
  1. Mathematics—Study and teaching (Middle school) 2. Mathematics—
Study and teaching (Secondary) I. LearningExpress (Organization)
  QA135.6.J86 2008
  510—dc22

                                2008021111

Printed in the United States of America

10 9 8 7 6 5 4 3 2

First Edition

For more information or to place an order, contact LearningExpress at:
  2 Rector Street
  26th Floor
  New York, NY 10006

Or visit us at:
  www.learnatest.com

CONTENTS

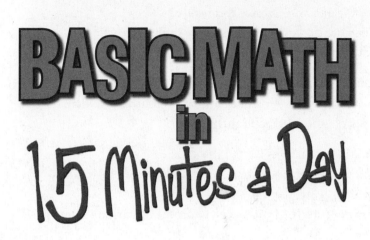

BASIC MATH
in
15 Minutes a Day

INTRODUCTION

DOES THE MERE MENTION of *mathematics* make you break out in a cold sweat? Do you have nightmares of being chased by flying geometric shapes or dark, mysterious variable equations? Have you ever lamented to your friends or teachers, "Will we *ever* use this stuff in real life?" Let's imagine a world without mathematics. Paradise, right? Don't smile just yet!

You wake up and look at your alarm clock. But, wait, there is no clock. Not only has the alarm clock not been invented (due to the lack of math), but there is no measurement system for keeping track of time! You step out of bed and stumble on the uneven bedroom floor. You see, without knowledge of geometry, your floor—and entire house—is crooked. You manage to make it to the kitchen and decide to make your great aunt's recipe for pancakes. But, wait a minute, what is the ratio of water to flour?

Before you even leave your home in the morning, you have, unwittingly, used math. And you did it without the nervous butterflies you feel in math class!

People have been using math for thousands of years, across various countries and continents. Everything in our society revolves around numbers.

Suppose you want to build a skateboard ramp in your backyard. You're going to need to use math to figure out the best possible ramp angle. Want to get pizza with friends? Math will help you know how many pizza pies you will need. Saving up your allowance for summer concert tickets? How much do you need to save each week? How far in advance do you need to save? This all requires math skills.

USING YOUR BOOK

Can you spare 15 minutes a day for a month? If so, *Basic Math in 15 Minutes a Day* can help you improve your math skills.

THE BOOK AT A GLANCE

What's in the book? First, there's this Introduction, in which you'll discover some things about this book. Next, there's a pretest that lets you find out what you already know about the topics in the book's lessons. You may be surprised by how much you already know. Then, there are 28 lessons. After the last one, there's a posttest. Take it to reveal how much you've learned and have improved your skills!

The lessons are divided into three sections:

- Number Boot Camp
- Basic Algebra—The Mysteries of Letters, Numbers, and Symbols
- Basic Geometry—All Shapes and Sizes

Each section has a series of lessons. Each lesson explains one math skill, and then presents questions so that you can practice that skill. And there are also math tips and trivia along the way! This book represents a progression of sets of math questions that build math skills. Thus, by design, this book is perfect for anybody seeking to attain better math skills.

The best thing about this book is that it puts the power in your hands. By dedicating just 15 minutes a day to the subjects in this book, you are moving toward a greater understanding of the world of math—and less sweaty palms!

THIS PRETEST HAS 30 multiple-choice questions about topics covered in the book's 28 lessons. Find out how much you already know about the topics, and then you'll discover what you still need to learn. Read each question carefully. Circle your answers if the book belongs to you. If it doesn't, write the numbers 1–30 on a paper and write your answers there. Try not to use a calculator. Instead, work out each problem on paper.

When you finish the test, check the answers beginning on page 10. Don't worry if you didn't get all the questions right. If you did, you wouldn't need this book! If you do have incorrect answers, check the numbers of the lessons listed with the correct answer. Then, go back and review those particular skills.

If you get a lot of questions right, you can probably spend less time using this book. If you get a lot wrong, you may need to spend a few more minutes a day to really improve your basic math skills.

PRETEST

1. Amber scored 3,487 points playing laser tag. Dale scored 5,012 points. About how many more points did Dale score than Amber?
   a. 500 points
   b. 1,000 points
   c. 1,500 points
   d. 3,000 points

2. Sonia checked the temperature for four major cities around the world. She found that it was −12° Celsius in Moscow, 4° Celsius in New York, −23° Celsius in Winnipeg, and 10° Celsius in Mexico City. Which of the following lists the cities in order from coldest temperature to warmest temperature?
   a. Winnipeg, Moscow, New York, Mexico City
   b. Moscow, Winnipeg, New York, Mexico City
   c. New York, Mexico City, Moscow, Winnipeg
   d. Mexico City, New York, Moscow, Winnipeg

3. Antonia used the commutative property of addition to quickly compute that $50 + 87 + 50$ is equal to 187. Which number sentence below illustrates an application of the commutative property that Antonia used?
   a. $50 + 87 + 50 = 137 + 50$
   b. $50 + 87 + 50 = 50 + (50 + 37) + 50$
   c. $50 + 87 + 50 = 50 + (87 + 50)$
   d. $50 + 87 + 50 = 50 + 50 + 87$

4. Evaluate: $4 - (3 - 2 \times 1)$
   a. −3
   b. −1
   c. 3
   d. 5

5. Harold has a cube with a number written on each side. The numbers 2, 3, 13, 29, 37, and 61 appear on the cube. When Harold rolls the cube, it will always land on a(n)
   a. prime number.
   b. composite number.
   c. odd number.
   d. mixed number.

6. Sammy fills $\frac{2}{7}$ of a bucket with sand. Jessie has an identical bucket and fills $\frac{3}{5}$ of it with sand. If Sammy pours all of the sand in his bucket into Jessie's bucket, what fraction of Jessie's bucket will be full?

    a. $\frac{5}{5}$

    b. $\frac{5}{12}$

    c. $\frac{21}{35}$

    d. $\frac{31}{35}$

7. Jim and Marco raced down Jim's driveway. It took Jim 6.38 seconds to reach the end of the driveway, while it took Marco 4.59 seconds. How much longer did it take Jim to finish the race?

    a. 0.79 seconds

    b. 1.79 seconds

    c. 1.89 seconds

    d. 2.79 seconds

8. In Mrs. Marsh's class, 3 out of every 7 students are boys. If there are 28 students in her class, how many boys are in her class?

    a. 3 boys

    b. 12 boys

    c. 14 boys

    d. 16 boys

9. Joel wants to purchase a CD for $16.25. The clerk tells him he must pay a sales tax equal to 8% of his purchase. How much sales tax must Joel pay?

    a. $1.30

    b. $1.63

    c. $2.03

    d. $13

10. Which number is the mean of the following data set?

    5, 2, 9, –1, 3

    a. 3

    b. 3.6

    c. 4

    d. 10

11. Carol works part time at the movie theater. Her schedule for the next three weeks lists the number of hours Carol will work each day.

Sunday	Monday	Tuesday	Wednesday	Thursday	Friday	Saturday
0	7	0	4	4	5	0
0	4	6	5	3	2	0
0	5	4	3	6	5	0

What is the median number of hours Carol will work over the next three weeks?

a. 0 hours

b. 3 hours

c. 4 hours

d. 5 hours

12. Tyson and Steve both collect skateboards. Tyson owns three less than seven times the number of skateboards Steve owns. If s represents the number of skateboards Steve owns, which of the following expressions represents the number of skateboards Tyson owns?

a. $7s$

b. $3 - 7s$

c. $7s - 3$

d. $\frac{1}{7}s + 3$

13. Sebastian finds that when $x = 7$, the expression $4x + 4$ has a value of which of the following?

a. 11

b. 24

c. 28

d. 32

14. Carla's dance squad organizes a car wash in the municipal parking lot. It costs them $250 to rent the lot, and they pay $35 for cleansers. If the squad charges $5 per car wash, how many cars must they wash to raise more money than their expenses?

a. 50 cars

b. 51 cars

c. 57 cars

d. 58 cars

15. What is the value of 2^5?

    a. 7

    b. 10

    c. 25

    d. 32

16. What is the number fourteen thousand written in scientific notation?

    a. 1.4×10^4

    b. 1.4×10^3

    c. 14,000

    d. 14×10^3

17. Which of the following equations is correct?

    a. $\sqrt{36} + \sqrt{64} = \sqrt{100}$

    b. $\sqrt{25} + \sqrt{16} = \sqrt{41}$

    c. $\sqrt{9} + \sqrt{25} = \sqrt{64}$

    d. There is no correct equation.

18. Lara is in charge of ticket sales for the school play. A ticket costs $3.75, and the school auditorium holds 658 people. What is the maximum amount of money Lara can collect for one night if she sells every seat in the auditorium?

    a. $175.47

    b. $1,974

    c. $2,467.50

    d. $24,675

19. Dominick lies down on his back to stretch his legs. He keeps his left leg straight along the floor and raises his right leg in the air as high as he can. Which of the following is most likely the measure of the angle made by Dominick's right leg and the floor?

    a. 10 degrees

    b. 70 degrees

    c. 180 degrees

    d. 270 degrees

20. Matt only likes shapes that have at least one pair of congruent sides. Matt likes all of the following EXCEPT

    a. squares.

    b. trapezoids.

    c. rhombuses.

    d. parallelograms.

21. The perimeter of a triangle is equal to the sum of the lengths of each side of the triangle. Roy draws an equilateral triangle, and every side is 6 centimeters long. What is the perimeter of Roy's triangle?

    a. 6 cm

    b. 12 cm

    c. 18 cm

    d. 216 cm

22. Pat paints a portrait that has a length of 30 inches and a width of 24 inches. What is the area of Pat's portrait? (Remember, the area of a rectangle is the length of the rectangle multiplied by the width of the rectangle.)

    a. 72 in.^{2}

    b. 108 in.^{2}

    c. 360 in.^{2}

    d. 720 in.^{2}

23. Which of the following shapes has four lines of symmetry?

    a. rectangle

    b. square

    c. right triangle

    d. isosceles trapezoid

24. Mischa draws two isosceles right triangles. Daryl looks at the triangles, and without measuring them, he can be sure that the triangles are

    a. similar.

    b. similar and congruent.

    c. congruent, but not similar.

    d. neither similar nor congruent.

25. Katie uses chalk to draw a circle on her driveway. If the radius of Katie's circle is 11 inches, what is the circumference of her circle? (Remember, the circumference of a circle is equal to 2πr, where r is the radius of the circle.)
  a. 11 in.
  b. 11π in.
  c. 22 in.
  d. 22π in.

✓ **26.** Theo builds a solid with exactly two congruent triangular faces. Theo has built a
  a. rectangular pyramid.
  b. triangular pyramid.
  c. cone.
  d. triangular prism.

27. Gary makes a diorama out of a shoebox. The shoebox has a width of 6 inches, a length of 12 inches, and a height of 5 inches. What is the volume of Gary's diorama? (Remember, the volume of a rectangular prism can be found by multiplying the prism's length by its width by its height.)
  a. 72 in.^{3}
  b. 216 in.^{3}
  c. 360 in.^{3}
  d. 432 in.^{3}

28. An empty cylindrical can has a height of 4 inches and a base with a radius of 1.5 inches. Melanie fills the can with water. What is the volume of the water Melanie pours into the can?
  a. 9π cubic inches
  b. 6.5π cubic inches
  c. 6π cubic inches
  d. 5.5π cubic inches

29. A cube with sides of length 4 centimeters has a surface area of 96 square centimeters. If the length of each side of the cube was doubled, what would be the surface area of the resulting cube?
  a. 192 square centimeters
  b. 768 square centimeters
  c. 384 square centimeters
  d. 2,304 square centimeters

30. Gerald draws two points on a grid: one at (8,15) and one at (3,3). What is the distance between Gerald's points?

a. 5 units

b. $\sqrt{119}$ units

c. 12 units

d. 13 units

ANSWERS

1. **c.** The question asks you to find "about" how many more points Dale scored than Amber. The word *about* signals estimation, and the phrase *how many more* tells you that you need to subtract. First, round each player's score to the nearest hundred.

   To round a number to the hundreds place, begin by looking at the digit in the tens place. If it is less than 5, round down; if it is greater than or equal to 5, round up.

   There is an "8" in the tens place of 3,487. Because 8 is greater than 5, round 3,487 up to the nearest hundred: 3,500. There is a "1" in the tens place of 5,012. Round 5,012 to 5,000.

   Finally, subtract:

   5,000 − 3,500 = 1,500

   Choice **c**, 1,500, is about how many more points Dale scored than Amber.

2. **a.** The city with the coldest temperature is Winnipeg, because −23 is less than −12, 4, and 10. Remember, the more negative a number is, the smaller its value. Only choice **a** begins with Winnipeg, so it is the correct answer.

3. **d.** The commutative property of addition says that you can change the order of addends in an expression without changing their sum; that is, $a + b = b + a$. In this equation, if you let $a = 50$ and $b = 87$, the commutative property states that $87 + 50 = 50 + 87$. Therefore, by applying the commutative property to the last two terms of the expression, you can write $50 + 87 + 50$ as $50 + 50 + 87$.

4. c. Use the order of operations to simplify this expression. Start inside the parentheses and multiply 2 and 1. Next, find the difference of the terms inside the parentheses. Finally, find the difference between 4 and 1. The steps in simplifying are shown here:

$$4-(3-2\times 1)$$
$$=4-(3-2)$$
$$=4-(1)$$
$$=4-1$$
$$=3$$

Choices **a**, **b**, and **d** are not equal to 3, so they are not correct. If you chose any of these answer choices, review the steps to see where you might have gone wrong. There are several places where an error might have occurred. Did you remember to perform the multiplication first? Did you remember to observe the parentheses?

Choice **a** represents the expression $4-3\times 2-1$.

Choice **b** represents the expression $4-3-2\times 1$.

If you selected choice **d**, you may have been evaluating the expression $4+(3-2\times 1)$.

5. a. The numbers written on the cube are divisible only by themselves and one. This means that they are all prime numbers.

6. d. After Sammy pours his sand into Jessie's bucket, his bucket represents the sum of his sand and Jessie's sand. Add the fraction that represents Sammy's sand, $\frac{2}{7}$, to the fraction that represents Jessie's sand, $\frac{3}{5}$:

$$\frac{2}{7}+\frac{3}{5}=$$

Before you can add fractions, you must find a common denominator. A common denominator of 7 and 5 is 35, because both 7 and 5 are divisible by 35.

Convert each fraction to 35ths. Multiply the numerator and denominator of $\frac{2}{7}$ by 5, and multiply the numerator and denominator of $\frac{3}{5}$ by 7:

$$\frac{2}{7}\times\frac{5}{5}=\frac{10}{35}$$
$$\frac{3}{5}\times\frac{7}{7}=\frac{21}{35}$$

Now that you have common denominators, add the numerators to find the sum of the fractions:

$$\frac{10}{35}+\frac{21}{35}=\frac{31}{35}$$

Jessie's bucket is $\frac{31}{35}$ full, choice **d**.

7. b. To find how much longer it took Jim to finish the race, subtract Marco's time from Jim's time:

$$6.38 - 4.59 = 1.79 \text{ seconds}$$

8. b. Use a proportion to solve this problem. If $\frac{3}{7}$ of Mrs. Marsh's students are boys, x of 28 students are boys:

$$\frac{3}{7} = \frac{x}{28}$$

Cross multiply:

$$7x = 84$$

Next, divide both sides by 7:

$$x = 12$$

So, 12 out of 28 students are boys, choice **b.**

9. a. Begin by writing 8% as a decimal. A percent is a number out of 100; 8% is 8 out of 100, or 0.08. To find 8% of $16.25, multiply $16.25 by 0.08:

$$\$16.25 \times 0.08 = \$1.30$$

10. b. The mean is the average of the numbers in a numeric data set. An average is equal to the sum of a set of numbers divided by the number of members of that set. Therefore, the mean of this set of numbers can be calculated as shown:

$$\frac{5 + 2 + 9 + (-1) + 3}{5} = \frac{18}{5} = 3.6$$

11. c. The median of a data set is the piece of data that occurs right in the middle after the data is put in numerical order. To find the median number of hours Carol will work over the next three weeks, put the number of hours she works each day in order and choose the number in the middle:

0, 0, 0, 0, 0, 0, 0, 2, 3, 3, **4**, 4, 4, 4, 5, 5, 5, 5, 6, 6, 7

There are 21 days on the schedule, so the middle number is the eleventh number shown above, 4. The median number of hours Carol will work is 4, choice **c.**

12. c. You are looking for an expression that is equal to the number of skateboards Tyson owns in terms of s, the number of skateboards Steve owns. Tyson owns three less than seven times the number of skateboards Steve owns. Because Steve owns s skateboards, seven times that is $7s$. Tyson owns three less than that amount. Subtract 3 from $7s$:

$$7s - 3$$

13. d. To evaluate this expression, replace the x with its value, 7:

$$4(7) + 4$$
$$= 28 + 4$$
$$= 32$$

14. d. The amount of money Carla's dance squad raises from washing cars must be greater than the amount of money it cost them to hold the car wash. First, find their total expenses. Renting the lot costs $250 and the cleansers cost $35. Add those figures to find the total expenses:

$250 + $35 = $285

Carla's dance squad must collect more than $285. If the number of cars washed is represented by c, then the inequality $5c > 285$ can be used to determine how many cars must be washed for the dance squad to raise more money than its expenses.

The dance squad earns $5 per car. Divide $285 by $5 to find the number of cars the squad must wash to meet its expenses:

$285 ÷ $5 = 57

$c > 57$

If the dance squad washes 57 cars, choice **c**, it will raise enough money to meet its expenses. However, to raise *more* money than its expenses, the squad must wash more than 57 cars. Only choice **d**, 58 cars, is greater than 57.

If the dance squad's total expenses were only $250, then 50 cars (choice **a**) would be the number of cars it would have to wash to raise enough money to pay for renting the lot, and choice **b**, 51 cars, would be the number of cars it would have to wash to raise more money than its rent.

15. d. The expression 2^5 represents 2 used as a factor five times:

$2 \times 2 \times 2 \times 2 \times 2 = 32.$

16. a. Scientific notation expresses a number as the product of a number between 1 and 10, including 1 and 10, and a power of ten. To write fourteen thousand in scientific notation, first write it in standard form, 14,000. Next, start at the far right of the number (where the decimal point lies) and move the decimal point four places to the left. This gives you 1.4, which is a number between 1 and 10, and the first factor in the number. Then, write the second factor as a power of ten. Because you moved the decimal point four places to the left, you can write 10 raised to the fourth power. The number in scientific notation is 1.4×10^4.

17. c. First, when you are finding the square root of a number, ask yourself, "What number times itself equals the given number?" Next, to get the answer to this problem, you can figure out each equation: It's not **a** because $\sqrt{36} = 6$, $\sqrt{64} = 8$, and $\sqrt{100} = 10$, and $6 + 8 = 14$, not 10. It's not **b** because $\sqrt{25} = 5$, $\sqrt{16} = 4$, and $\sqrt{41}$ is about 6.4, and $5 + 4 = 9$, not 6.4. It is **c** because $\sqrt{9} = 3$, $\sqrt{25} = 5$, and $\sqrt{64} = 8$, and $3 + 5 = 8$.

18. c. The maximum amount of money Lara can collect is equal to the price of one ticket, $3.75, multiplied by the total number of seats in the auditorium, 658:

$3.75 \times 658 = \$2,467.50$

19. b. Dominick's left leg is straight along the floor, so he will be able to raise his leg somewhere between 0 and 90 degrees. It would be very difficult for Dominick to raise his leg more than 90 degrees, but it would be easy for him to raise his leg at least 45 degrees. Because Dominick is trying to raise his leg as high as he can, the angle between his leg and the floor is probably between 45 and 90 degrees. Only choice **b**, 70 degrees, is between 45 and 90 degrees.

20. b. Consider each answer choice.

A square, choice **a**, has two pairs of congruent sides—in fact, all four sides of a square are congruent.

A trapezoid, choice, **b**, has one pair of parallel sides, but unless it is an isosceles trapezoid, it has no pairs of congruent sides. Choice **b** is the correct answer.

A rhombus, choice **c**, has two pairs of congruent sides. Like a square, all four sides are congruent.

A parallelogram, choice **d**, also has two pairs of congruent sides.

21. c. The formula for perimeter is given in the question: Add the lengths of each side of the triangle to find the perimeter of the triangle. Roy draws an equilateral triangle, which is a triangle with three sides that are all the same length. All three sides are 6 cm long:

6 cm + 6 cm + 6 cm = 18 cm

22. d. Here is the formula for the area of a rectangle:

Area of a rectangle = (length of the rectangle)(width of the rectangle)
Substitute the length and width of the rectangle into the formula:

Area of a rectangle = (30 in.)(24 in.)
Area of a rectangle = 720 in.^{2}

23. b. Only a square has four lines of symmetry: one vertical, one horizontal, and two diagonal lines of symmetry.

24. a. A right triangle is a triangle with a 90-degree angle. An isosceles triangle is a triangle with two congruent angles. An isosceles right triangle has a 90-degree angle and two congruent angles. Because a triangle can have only one 90-degree angle, that means that the other two angles must be congruent. A triangle has 180 degrees, so an isosceles right triangle has angles that measure 90 degrees, 45 degrees, and 45 degrees.

All isosceles right triangles have the same angle measures, so all isosceles right triangles are similar. Similar triangles are triangles that have the same angle measures. Therefore, without measuring Mischa's isosceles right triangles, Daryl knows the two triangles are similar.

25. d. The formula for circumference is given in the question:

Circumference of a circle = $(2)(\pi)$(radius of the circle)

Substitute the value of the radius into the formula:

Circumference of a circle = $(2)(\pi)(11 \text{ in.})$

Circumference of a circle = 22π in.

26. d. Consider each answer choice.

Choice **a**, a rectangular pyramid, is a three-dimensional solid with five faces, four of which are triangles. Theo's solid has only two triangular faces, so choice **a** is incorrect.

Choice **b**, a triangular pyramid, is a three-dimensional solid with four faces, all of which are triangles. Theo's solid has only two triangular faces, so choice **b** is incorrect.

Choice **c**, a cone, is a three-dimensional solid with two faces, neither of which is a triangle, so choice **c** is incorrect.

Choice **d**, a triangular prism, is a three-dimensional solid with five faces, including three rectangular faces that are congruent and two triangular faces that are congruent. Theo has built a triangular prism.

27. c. Remember the formula for the volume of a rectangular prism:

Volume of a rectangular prism = (length)(width)(height)

Substitute the length, width, and height of the diorama into the formula:

Volume of a rectangular prism = $(12 \text{ in.})(6 \text{ in.})(5 \text{ in.})$

Volume of a rectangular prism = 360 in.^3

28. a. You used the formula $V = \pi r^2 h$, where r is the radius of the base and h is the height of the cylinder: $\pi(1.5^2)4 = \pi \times 2.25 \times 4$, which equals 9π.

29. c. The new cube would have sides of length 8 centimeters.

$6(8^2) = 384$

30. d. Use the distance formula to find the distance between two points:

Distance = $\sqrt{(x_2 - x_1)^2 + (y_2 - y_1)^2}$

Plug the coordinates of Gerald's points into the formula:

Distance = $\sqrt{(8-3)^2 + (15-3)^2}$

Distance = $\sqrt{(5)^2 + (12)^2}$

Distance = $\sqrt{25 + 144}$

Distance = $\sqrt{169}$

Distance = 13 units

S E C T I O N 1

number boot camp

WHAT DO YOU think of when you hear the phrase *boot camp*? Maybe your mind is swimming with images of men and women in camouflage completing grueling physical tasks as drill sergeants bark commands at them.

Well, this section is a different kind of boot camp—one in which you will strengthen your mind by completing basic math drills. These drills will start with the basics, using different types of numbers to later show you how to use these numbers in order to perform arithmetic operations. Along the way, you'll leap over absolute value, crawl under divisibility, and maneuver around graphs that display data. And when you're done with this number boot camp, you'll have a solid basic math foundation!

This section will introduce you to basic number concepts, including:

- numbers
- operations
- absolute value
- order of operations
- factors
- fractions
- decimals
- ratios
- proportions
- percents
- measures of central tendency
- graphs

1

numbers, operations, and absolute value

Arithmetic is numbers you squeeze from your head to your hand to your pencil to your paper till you get the answer.
—CARL SANDBURG (1878–1967)

In this lesson, you will discover the ins and outs of integers. Think you already know these math players? This lesson will teach you some shortcuts to operations with integers. You'll also learn facts about zero, absolute value, and number properties.

NUMBERS, NUMBERS, NUMBERS. Before you can begin to build your basic math skills, you'll need to understand the different types of numbers.

Integers are the numbers that you see on a number line.

$$\longleftarrow \quad | \quad | \quad | \quad | \quad | \quad | \quad | \quad | \quad | \quad | \quad | \quad \longrightarrow$$
$$-5 \; -4 \; -3 \; -2 \; -1 \; \; 0 \; \; 1 \; \; 2 \; \; 3 \; \; 4 \; \; 5$$

This does not include fractions, such as $\frac{1}{2}$, $\frac{3}{4}$, and $\frac{8}{9}$, or decimals like 1.125, 2.4, and 9.56. No fractions or decimals are allowed in the world of integers. *What a wonderful world*, you say. No troublesome fractions and pesky decimals.

Positive integers are integers that are larger than zero. Negative integers are smaller than zero. When you are working with negative and positive integers, try to think about a number line. The following number lines will help you see addition and subtraction from different points on the number line.

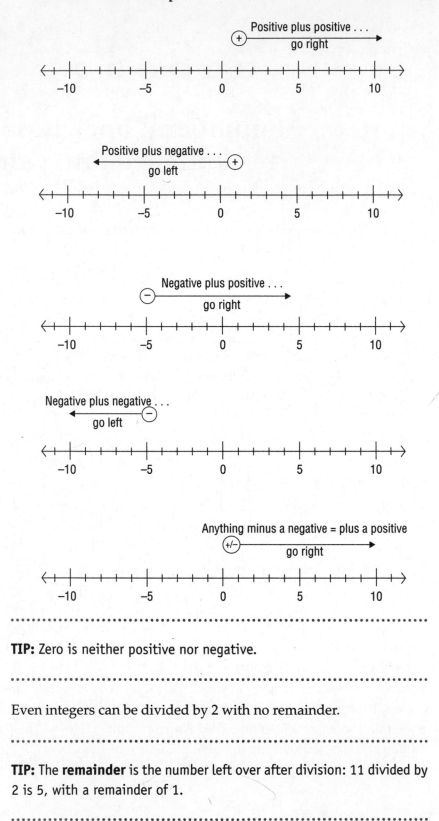

TIP: Zero is neither positive nor negative.

Even integers can be divided by 2 with no remainder.

TIP: The **remainder** is the number left over after division: 11 divided by 2 is 5, with a remainder of 1.

Even integers include –4, –2, 0, 2, and 4. Odd integers cannot be divided by 2 with no remainder. These would include –3, –1, 1, and 3.

....

TIP: Let's examine the properties of zero:

The sum of any number and zero is that number: $0 + 7 = 7$.
The product of any number and zero is zero: $0 \times 7 = 0$.

....

ABSOLUTE VALUE

If you look at a point on a number line, measure its distance from zero, and consider that value as positive, you have just found the number's absolute value. Let's take the absolute value of 3.

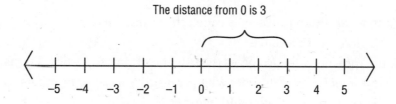

The distance from 0 is 3

The absolute value of 3, written as |3|, is 3.
Next, let's calculate the absolute value of –3.

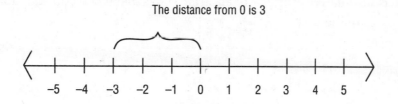

The distance from 0 is 3

The absolute value of –3, written as |–3|, is also 3.

PRACTICE 1

Find the absolute values.

1. $|156| =$

2. $|-97| =$

3. $-|-13| =$

4. $|74| + |-23| =$

5. $|35| - |-12| =$

ADDING AND SUBTRACTING INTEGERS

The result in an addition problem is called the **sum**. The result in a subtraction problem is called the **difference**.

Adding integers often involves the use of certain properties. The **associative property of addition** states that when you add a series of numbers, you can regroup the numbers any way you'd like:

$$1 + (9 + 7) = (1 + 9) + 7 = (1 + 7) + 9$$

The **commutative property of addition** states that when you add numbers, order doesn't matter:

$$8 + 2 = 2 + 8$$

MULTIPLYING AND DIVIDING INTEGERS

The result in a multiplication problem is called a **product**. The result in a division problem is called a **quotient**.

The product of two integers with the same sign (+ and + or − and −) is always positive. The product of two integers with different signs (+ and −) is always negative.

$3 \times 4 = 12$

$-3 \times -4 = 12$

$-3 \times 4 = -12$

$3 \times -4 = -12$

Likewise, the quotient of two integers with the same sign (+ and + or − and −) is always positive. The quotient of two integers with the different signs (+ and −) is always negative.

$4 \div 2 = 2$

$-4 \div -2 = 2$

$-4 \div 2 = -2$

$4 \div -2 = -2$

When multiplying integers, you will often use the same properties you used with the addition of integers. The **associative property of multiplication** states that when you are multiplying a series of numbers, you can regroup the numbers any way you'd like:

$2 \times (5 \times 9) = (2 \times 5) \times 9 = (2 \times 9) \times 5$

The **commutative property of multiplication** states that when you multiply integers, order doesn't matter:

$6 \times 5 = 5 \times 6$

PRACTICE 2

To practice your arithmetic skills, take the following drill without a calculator. Then, look at the trivia question at the end of the lesson. Match your answer and its corresponding letter to the number answers that complete the trivia answer. (If you need to, you can rewrite these questions in a different form—stacking addition problems or using long division, for example.)

1. $17 + -4 = W$

2. $174 + 58 = L$

3. $1{,}023 + 75 = E$

4. $99 - 16 = C$

5. $-3 - -5 = I$

6. $-59 - 18 = L$

7. $9 \times 7 = A$

8. $-15 \times -3 = S$

9. $100 \times -3 = O$

10. $125 \div 25 = R$

11. $-81 \div -9 = R$

12. $-258 \div 3 = L$

What famous writer called the four branches of arithmetic "Ambition, Distraction, Uglification, and Derision"?

$\overline{}$ $\overline{}$ $\overline{}$ $\overline{}$ $\overline{}$
-86 1,098 13 2 45

$\overline{}$ $\overline{}$ $\overline{}$ $\overline{}$ $\overline{}$ $\overline{}$ $\overline{}$
83 63 5 9 -300 -77 232

ANSWERS

Practice 1

1. $|156| = 156$
2. $|-97| = 97$
3. $-|-13| = -13$
4. $|74| + |-23| = 97$
5. $|35| - |-12| = 23$

Practice 2

1. $17 + -4 = 13$
2. $174 + 58 = 232$
3. $1{,}023 + 75 = 1{,}098$
4. $99 - 16 = 83$
5. $-3 - -5 = 2$
6. $-59 - 18 = -77$
7. $9 \times 7 = 63$
8. $-15 \times -3 = 45$
9. $100 \times -3 = -300$
10. $125 \div 25 = 5$
11. $-81 \div -9 = 9$
12. $-258 \div 3 = -86$

What famous writer called the four branches of arithmetic "Ambition, Distraction, Uglification, and Derision"?

L E W I S

C A R R O L L

(This quote is from his famous book, *Alice in Wonderland*.)

order of operations

The chief forms of beauty are order and symmetry and definiteness, which the mathematical sciences demonstrate in a specific degree.

—ARISTOTLE (384–322 B.C.)

Please excuse my dear aunt Sally, and you'll breeze through this lesson about the order of operations. Think PEMDAS is overrated? Think again!

WHEN YOU GET a messy mathematical expression that involves every operation under the sun, you must remember to perform the operations in the correct order. This order, often referred to as PEMDAS, is:

Parentheses → Exponents → Multiplication and Division (from left to right) → Addition and Subtraction (from left to right)

First, perform any math operations located inside parentheses.

• •

TIP: Often, in expressions, there are grouping symbols—usually shown as parentheses—which are used to make a mathematical statement clear.

• •

Then, calculate any exponents.

TIP: An **exponent** is a number that tells you how many times a number is multiplied by itself: $2^3 = 2 \times 2 \times 2$. For more on exponents, see Lesson 13.

Next, solve the multiplication and division from left to right. Finally, complete any addition or subtraction from left to right.

PEMDAS is often remembered with the phrase *Please Excuse My Dear Aunt Sally.* You may want to create your own personal sentence to remember the order of operations.

You may be wondering why you really need to follow the order of operations. Does it really matter? Let's look at what happens when you ignore PEMDAS and attack a problem in order of appearance:

$9 + 8 \times 2 - 3 \times 2$

$17 \times 2 - 3 \times 2$

$34 - 3 \times 2$

31×2

62

Is this answer correct? Because you ignored PEMDAS, this is not the right answer. No worries—now proceed in the correct order. There are no parentheses or exponents, so we need to do any multiplication or division first from left to right.

$9 + 8 \times 2 - 3 \times 2$

$9 + 16 - 3 \times 2$

$9 + 16 - 6$

Now, complete the addition and subtraction from left to right.

$9 + 16 - 6$

$25 - 6$

19

Wow—without using the order of operations, the answer wasn't even close to the actual value! Remember, take your time and carry out each operation in the correct order.

Let's look at another example.

$$2^2 + (6-5) - (3+3) \times 3 =$$

Begin by completing any work inside the parentheses.

$$(6-5) = 1 \text{ and } (3+3) = 6$$

The original problem is now as follows:

$$2^2 + 1 - 6 \times 3 =$$

Calculate the exponent: $2^2 = 4$. Now, you can further simplify the problem.

$$4 + 1 - 6 \times 3 =$$

The next stage of PEMDAS, the MD, indicates that you should do all the multiplication and division from left to right. There is no division to worry about, but there is multiplication: 6×3. This equals 18. So, your problem is now:

$$4 + 1 - 18$$

You're almost there! Perform all addition and subtraction. Remember to do this from left to right.

$$4 + 1 = 5 \text{ and } 5 - 18 = -13$$

So, $2^2 + (6-5) - (3+3) \times 3 = -13$.

PRACTICE 1

Use the order of operations to find the answers. Show your work.

1. $8 + 15 \times 3 =$

2. $7 + 24 \div 6 \times 10 =$

3. $(36 + 64) \div (18 - 20) =$

ABSOLUTE VALUE AND PEMDAS

In Lesson 1, you learned the meaning of the absolute value. When using the order of operations, the absolute value symbol is treated at the same level as parentheses.

Try this out:

$5 \times |{-}13 + 3|$

First, evaluate the expression inside the absolute value symbol:

$5 \times |{-}10|$

Now, evaluate the absolute value:

$|{-}10| = 10$, so $5 \times 10 = 50$

....

TIP: If your calculator has parentheses keys, then your calculator most likely will perform the correct order of operations. Check your calculator with these examples to see if your calculator performs the correct order of operations.

To evaluate $16 - 100 \div 5$, enter the numbers as they appear. Your calculator should show a result of −4.

To evaluate $48 \div (4 + 2)$, again enter the numbers as they appear. (Don't forget about the opening and closing parentheses!) Your calculator should show a result of 8.

....

PRACTICE 2

1. $100 \div 5 + |-5 \times 3| =$

2. $5 \times -|9| =$

3. $99 \div |-33| =$

ANSWERS

Practice 1

1. In this problem, there are no parentheses or exponents, so evaluate multiplication first: 8 + 45. Now, perform the addition: 53.
2. Again, there are no parentheses or exponents, so evaluate multiplication and division from left to right. First, do the division: 7 + 4 × 10. Next, perform multiplication: 7 + 40. Finally, perform addition: 47.
3. First, evaluate parentheses, from left to right: 100 ÷ –2. Now, do the division: –50.

Practice 2

1. The absolute value symbol serves as a grouping symbol, and grouping symbols are evaluated first: |–5 × 3| = 15. Now, divide 5 into 100 to get 20. Finally, add 20 + 15 = 35.
2. –|9| is equal to the opposite of the absolute value of 9, or –9: 5 × –9 = –45.
3. |–33| is equal to 33. What times 33 equals 99? Your answer should be 3.

factors and divisibility

The control of large numbers is possible and like unto
that of small numbers, if we subdivide them.

—SUN TZE (544–496 B.C.)

This chapter will show you interesting facts about factors and factorization, including shortcuts and clues. You will also discover how to find the GCF and LCM—and what these letters stand for!

A NUMBER IS a factor of a second number if it can be divided into the second number without leaving a remainder. Let's look at the factors of 12: 1, 2, 3, 4, 6, and 12. The number 12 can be divided by each of these numbers without there being a remainder.

$12 \div 1 = 12$

$12 \div 2 = 6$

$12 \div 3 = 4$

$12 \div 4 = 3$

$12 \div 6 = 2$

$12 \div 12 = 1$

If you start with 1 and the number itself when you write down factor pairs, you won't forget any of them. For 12, the factor pairs are as follows:

1 and 12

2 and 6

3 and 4

DIVISIBILITY SHORTCUTS

If a number is a factor of a given number, the given number is divisible by the factor. There are a few simple rules that will help you quickly determine divisibility and factor problems.

- An integer is divisible by 2 if its ones digit is divisible by 2.
- An integer is divisible by 3 if the sum of its digits is divisible by 3.
- An integer is divisible by 4 if its last two digits form a number divisible by 4.
- An integer is divisible by 5 if its ones digit is either 0 or 5.
- An integer is divisible by 6 if it is divisible by both 2 and 3.
- An integer is divisible by 9 if the sum of its digits is divisible by 9.
- An integer is divisible by 10 if its ones digit is 0.

PRACTICE 1

Circle the numbers divisible by 9. Underline the numbers divisible by 2. Draw a square around the numbers divisible by 6.

4	25
5	29
7	36
12	44
13	53
17	81
21	90

PRIME FACTORIZATION

When an integer greater than 1 has exactly two factors (1 and itself), it is a **prime number**. Examples of prime numbers include 2, 3, 5, 7, 11, 13, 17, 19, 23, and 29. Note that the opposite (negative version) of these numbers are also prime. For example, the factors of –23 are 1, –23, –1, and 23. Thus, –23 is prime because it has exactly two positive factors: 1 and 23.

TIP: The number 2 is the only even prime number.

When an integer greater than 1 has more than two factors, it is called a **composite number**.

The numbers 0 and 1 are neither prime nor composite. Zero has an infinite number of factors. The number 1, on the other hand, has one factor—itself.

When a number is expressed as a product of factors that are all prime, that expression is called the **prime factorization** of the number.

GREATEST COMMON FACTOR

The greatest of all the factors common to two or more numbers is called the **greatest common factor (GCF)**.

Let's find the common factor of 24 and 40.

First, find the factors of 24: 1, 2, 3, 4, 6, 8, 12, and 24.

Now, find the factors of 40: 1, 2, 4, 5, 8, 10, 20, and 40.

What is the greatest factor common to both 24 and 40? The greatest common factor to both is 8.

LEAST COMMON MULTIPLE

A multiple of a number is the product of that number and any whole number. The least of the common multiples of two or more numbers, excluding 0, is called the **least common multiple (LCM)**.

Let's determine the least common multiple of 4, 6, and 8.

First, find the multiples of 4: 4, 8, 12, 16, 20, **24**, 28, 32, 36, 40, and so on.

Now, find the multiples of 6: 6, 12, 18, **24**, 30, 36, 42, 48, 54, 60, and so on.

Finally, find the multiples of 8: 8, 16, **24**, 32, 40, 48, 56, 64, 72, 80, and so on.

If you look at 4 and 6 only, you may mistakenly pick 12 as the LCM of all three numbers. But, 12 is not a multiple of 8. Instead, the first multiple found in all three numbers is 24.

PRACTICE 2

1. What is the prime factorization of 60?

2. Find the greatest common factor of 20 and 30.

3. Find the greatest common factor of 63 and 81.

4. Find the least common multiple of 63 and 81.

ANSWERS

Practice 1

Circle the numbers divisible by 9. Underline the numbers divisible by 2. Draw a square around the numbers divisible by 6.

<u>4</u>

5

7

☐12☐

13

17

21

25

29

Ⓢ36Ⓢ

<u>44</u>

53

⑧1

Ⓢ90Ⓢ

Practice 2

1. $2 \times 2 \times 3 \times 5$

2. The prime factorization of 20 is $2 \times 2 \times 5$. The prime factorization of $30 = 2 \times 3 \times 5$. Because 2 and 5 are prime factors of both 20 and 30, the greatest common factor is 2 times 5, which is 10.

3. Factors of 63: 1, 3, 7, **9**, 21, 63
Factors of 81: 1, 3, **9**, 27, 81
All factors have been listed. The largest one in common between 63 and 81 is 9.

4. Multiples of 63: 63, 126, 189, 252, 315, 378, 441, 504, **567**
Multiples of 81: 81, 162, 243, 324, 405, 486, **567**
Multiples are listed until one is found in common. The least common multiple of 63 and 81 is 567.

fractions

Five out of four people have trouble with fractions.
—STEVEN WRIGHT (1955–)

This chapter explores the different types of fractions and how to order them. A discussion on how to perform operations of these types of numbers comes later.

FRACTIONS ARE USED to represent parts of a whole. You can think of the fraction bar as meaning "out of" or "divided by."

$\frac{1}{2}$ means 1 out of 2 or 1 divided by 2.
$\frac{5}{8}$ means 5 out of 8 or 5 divided by 8.

Although you may call the top part of the fraction the "top" and the bottom part of a fraction the "bottom," their technical names are **numerator** and **denominator**.

You are never allowed to have a zero in the denominator. Anything over zero is undefined. In other words, this is not a real number and should never be done.

A **proper fraction** has a numerator that is smaller than its denominator:

$\frac{9}{10}, \frac{19}{20}, \frac{99}{100}$

Improper fractions have numerators that are bigger than their denominators:

$$\frac{15}{10}, \frac{45}{20}, \frac{100}{50}$$

A **mixed number** is a number that is represented as an integer and a fraction. The following are all mixed numbers:

$$7\frac{3}{4}, 8\frac{1}{2}, 2\frac{6}{8}$$

To change a mixed number into an improper fraction, follow these steps:

1. Multiply the denominator of the fraction by the number.
2. Add that sum to the numerator.
3. Put that amount over the original denominator.

Try these steps with $7\frac{3}{4}$.

Step 1: $4 \times 7 = 28$

Step 2: $28 + 3 = 31$

Step 3: $\frac{31}{4}$

$\frac{31}{4}$ is equal to $7\frac{3}{4}$. The only difference is that $\frac{31}{4}$ is easier to work with.

Negative fractions are fractions that have a minus sign in front of them. Just like integers and numbers, a fraction multiplied by a negative also becomes negative. For example:

$$-1 \times \frac{1}{2} = -\frac{1}{2}$$

A fraction can be considered negative if either its numerator or denominator is negative. In this example, it might look like only the numerator is negative, but in fact, the entire fraction is receiving the negative value.

When a fraction receives any type of sign, particularly the negative sign, it can appear in three different places—in the numerator, denominator, or right before the fraction:

$$\frac{-1}{2} \qquad \frac{1}{-2} \qquad -\frac{1}{2}$$

Any way you write it, you are indicating the same number. No matter where the negative is placed within the fraction, it has the same value.

ADDING AND SUBTRACTING LIKE FRACTIONS

To add or subtract fractions, the denominators have to match. To add fractions with like denominators, just add the numerators. To subtract fractions with like denominators, just subtract the numerators.

$$\frac{30}{50} + \frac{15}{50} = \frac{45}{50}$$
$$\frac{4}{5} - \frac{1}{5} = \frac{3}{5}$$

ADDING AND SUBTRACTING UNLIKE FRACTIONS

To find the sum or difference of two fractions with unlike denominators, rename the fractions with a common denominator. Then, add or subtract and simplify your answer.

Let's put this into practice. What would $\frac{4}{5} - \frac{3}{4}$ equal?

To subtract these fractions, you first need to find a common denominator. A good method for finding a common denominator is the bowtie method. In the bowtie method, multiply the two denominators. Then, multiply up and diagonally to get the numerators. You will be left with two fractions that have the same denominator.

$$\frac{4}{5} \quad \frac{3}{4}$$

$$\frac{16}{20} - \frac{15}{20} = \frac{1}{20}$$

MULTIPLYING FRACTIONS

To multiply fractions, multiply the numerators, then multiply the denominators, and finally simplify, if possible and necessary.

Try this with $\frac{4}{5} \times \frac{2}{3}$. First, multiply the numerators: $4 \times 2 = 8$. Now, do the same with the denominators: $5 \times 3 = 15$. So, $\frac{4}{5} \times \frac{2}{3} = \frac{8}{15}$, which cannot be simplified.

If you are asked to find the fraction of a number, multiply that number by the fraction. In other words, *of* means ×, or "multiply." For example, $\frac{1}{4}$ of 16 means $\frac{1}{4} \times 16 = 4$.

DIVIDING FRACTIONS

To divide one fraction by another, you need to flip the second fraction and then multiply the fractions. This flip of the second fraction is called the **multiplicative inverse** of a number or the **reciprocal**.

It's easier than it may seem. Try this problem:

$$\frac{3}{5} \div \frac{2}{3} =$$

First, find the reciprocal of $\frac{2}{3}$: $\frac{3}{2}$. Now, multiply: $\frac{3}{5} \times \frac{3}{2} = \frac{9}{10}$.

COMPARING FRACTIONS

Sometimes, you may need to find the greatest fractions or put fractions in order from least to greatest or from greatest to least.

Let's try putting the following fractions from least to greatest:

$$\frac{2}{3}, \frac{3}{4}, \frac{1}{3}, \frac{2}{4}$$

To do this, you should first give all the fractions a common denominator. The least common multiple of 3 and 4 is 12, so let's make 12 the new denominator for all four fractions:

$$\frac{8}{12}, \frac{9}{12}, \frac{4}{12}, \frac{6}{12}$$

All that's left to do is to put the numbers in order from least to greatest:

$$\frac{4}{12}, \frac{6}{12}, \frac{8}{12}, \frac{9}{12}$$

So, this means the order of the fractions from least to greatest would be $\frac{1}{3}, \frac{2}{4}, \frac{2}{3}$, and $\frac{3}{4}$.

PRACTICE 1

1. $\frac{4}{9} - \frac{7}{9} =$

2. $\frac{8}{15} + \frac{9}{30} =$

3. $2\frac{3}{4} - 3\frac{2}{4} =$

4. $\frac{7}{9} \times \frac{3}{4} =$

5. $4\frac{2}{3} \div 6 =$

6. $\frac{6}{11} + \frac{3}{11} =$

7. $\frac{1}{4} + \frac{2}{7} =$

8. $\frac{10}{17} - \frac{6}{17} =$

9. $\frac{3}{4} - \frac{2}{5} =$

10. $\frac{2}{3} \times \frac{9}{13} =$

11. Which fraction is greater, $\frac{5}{9}$ or $\frac{7}{12}$?

12 Convert $\frac{19}{5}$ to a mixed number.

13. Convert $6\frac{5}{8}$ to an improper fraction.

ANSWERS

1. The two fractions already have a common denominator, so combine the numerators, and keep the denominator. Then simplify: $\frac{4}{9} - \frac{7}{9} = \frac{4-7}{9} = -\frac{3}{9} \div \frac{3}{3} = -\frac{1}{3}$.

2. First, find a common denominator, the LCM of 15 and 30. The LCM is 30. Convert the first fraction to have a denominator of 30: $\frac{8}{15} \times \frac{2}{2} = \frac{16}{30}$. Now combine to get $\frac{16}{30} + \frac{9}{30} = \frac{25}{30} \div \frac{5}{5} = \frac{5}{6}$.

3. Change each mixed number to an improper fraction: $2\frac{3}{4} - 3\frac{2}{4} = \frac{11}{4} - \frac{14}{4}$. The fractions have the same denominator, so combine the numerators and keep the denominator: $\frac{11}{4} - \frac{14}{4} = \frac{11-14}{4} = -\frac{3}{4}$.

4. When you multiply fractions, multiply straight across and then simplify: $\frac{7}{9} \times \frac{3}{4} = \frac{21}{36} \div \frac{3}{3} = \frac{7}{12}$.

5. Change $4\frac{2}{3}$ and 6 to improper fractions. Then change the operation to multiply by the reciprocal of 6: $\frac{14}{3} \div \frac{6}{1} = \frac{14}{3} \times \frac{1}{6}$. Multiply the numerators and the denominators straight across and simplify: $\frac{14}{3} \times \frac{1}{6} = \frac{14 \times 1}{3 \times 6} = \frac{14}{18} \div \frac{2}{2} = \frac{7}{9}$.

6. These fractions are like fractions, because they have the same denominator. To add two like fractions, add the numerators of the fractions: $6 + 3 = 9$. The denominator of our answer is the same as the denominator of the two fractions that you are adding. Both fractions have a denominator of 11, so the denominator of our answer will be 11: $\frac{6}{11} + \frac{3}{11} = \frac{9}{11}$.

7. Because these fractions are unlike, you must find common denominators for them before adding. First, you find the least common multiple of 4 and 7:

   4: 4, 8, 12, 16, 20, 24, 28, 32, . . .
   7: 7, 14, 21, 28, 35, 42, 49, . . .

   The least common multiple of 4 and 7 is 28. Convert both fractions to a number over 28. Because $\frac{28}{4} = 7$, the new denominator of the fraction $\frac{1}{4}$ is seven times larger. The new numerator must also be seven times larger, so that the value of the fraction does not change: $1 \times 7 = 7$; $\frac{1}{4} = \frac{7}{28}$. Because $\frac{28}{7} = 4$, the new denominator of the fraction $\frac{2}{7}$ is four times larger. Multiply the numerator of the fraction by four: $2 \times 4 = 8$; $\frac{2}{7} = \frac{8}{28}$. Now that you have like fractions, you can add the numerators: $7 + 8 = 15$. Because the denominator of the fractions you are adding is 28, the denominator of our answer is 28: $\frac{7}{28} + \frac{8}{28} = \frac{15}{28}$.

8. These fractions are like fractions, so you can subtract the numerator of the second fraction from the numerator of the first fraction: $10 - 6 = 4$. The denominator of both fractions is 17, so the denominator of our answer is 17: $\frac{10}{17} - \frac{6}{17} = \frac{4}{17}$.

9. Because these fractions are unlike, you must find common denominators for them before subtracting. First, you find the least common multiple of 4 and 5:

   4: 4, 8, 12, 16, 20, 24, . . .
   5: 5, 10, 15, 20, 25, . . .

   The least common multiple of 4 and 5 is 20. Convert both fractions to a number over 20. Because $\frac{20}{4} = 5$, the new denominator of the fraction $\frac{3}{4}$ is five times larger. Therefore, the new numerator must also be five times larger, so that the value of the fraction does not change: $3 \times 5 = 15$; $\frac{3}{4} = \frac{15}{20}$. Because $\frac{20}{5} = 4$, the new denominator of the fraction $\frac{2}{5}$ is four times larger. Multiply the numerator of the fraction by four: $2 \times 4 = 8$; $\frac{2}{5} = \frac{8}{20}$. Now that you have like fractions, you can subtract the second numerator from the first numerator: $15 - 8 = 7$. The denominator of the fractions is 20, so the denominator of our answer is 20: $\frac{15}{20} - \frac{8}{20} = \frac{7}{20}$.

10. The product of two fractions is equal to the product of the numerators over the product of the denominators. Multiply the numerators: $2 \times 9 = 18$. Multiply the denominators: $3 \times 13 = 39$; $\frac{2}{3} \times \frac{9}{13} = \frac{18}{39}$. You can reduce your answer by dividing the numerator and denominator by their greatest common factor. The greatest common factor of 18 and 39 is 3: $\frac{18}{3} = 6$ and $\frac{39}{3} = 13$, so $\frac{18}{39} = \frac{6}{13}$.

11. First, list the factors of the numerator and the denominator. The factors of 16 are 1, 2, 4, 8, and 16, and the factors of 24 are 1, 2, 3, 4, 6, 8, 12, and 24. The greatest common factor (the largest number that is a factor of both 16 and 24) is 8. Divide the numerator and denominator of $\frac{16}{24}$ by 8: $\frac{16}{8} = 2$ and $\frac{24}{8} = 3$. $\frac{16}{24}$ reduces to $\frac{2}{3}$.

12. To convert an improper fraction to a mixed number, divide the numerator by the denominator: $19 \div 5 = 3$ with 4 left over. You express the remainder as a fraction. The improper fraction has a denominator of 5, so our remainder has a denominator of 5: $19 \div 5 = 3\frac{4}{5}$.

13. To convert a mixed number to an improper fraction, you begin by multiplying the whole number, 6, by the denominator of the fraction, 8: $6 \times 8 = 48$. Next, add to that product the numerator of the fraction: $48 + 5 = 53$. Finally, put that sum over the denominator of the fraction: $6\frac{5}{8} = \frac{53}{8}$.

decimals

Decimals have a point.
—AUTHOR UNKNOWN

In this lesson, you'll learn about the wonders of a simple decimal point, how to perform operations on decimals, and how to convert between decimals and fractions.

THE DECIMAL SYSTEM is a way to name numbers based on the powers of 10. The numbers to the right of the decimal point are fractional equivalents with denominators that are powers of ten. For example,

$0.1 = \frac{1}{10}$
$0.2 = \frac{2}{10}$
$0.3 = \frac{3}{10}$

Decimals are based on the place value of our number system where position from the decimal point has meaning:

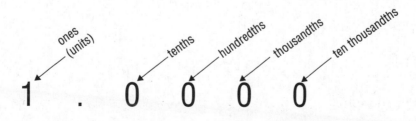

Note the pattern of how the names of the decimal places to the right of the decimal are similar to the names of the place values to the left of the decimal point. Keep the mental image of the decimal point pairing up with the "ones" place in order to easily remember the place value names.

The decimal number 1.52 is read as "one and fifty-two hundredths," or $1\frac{52}{100}$. The number 0.05 is read as "five hundredths," or $\frac{5}{100}$.

Decimal numbers are easy to compare and order, when you remember that the place value has meaning. In mathematics, 2.4 is the same number as 2.400 because both numbers represent "two and four tenths." A whole number is understood to have a decimal point to the right of the number. For example, 12 = 12. = 12.0 = 12.000. Each expression represents twelve with no remainder. To compare decimals, it is best to change each decimal into an equivalent decimal with the same number of decimal places.

Try ordering the numbers from least to greatest: .016, 0.7, .203, .75

Because some of the numbers have three places to the right of the decimal point, change each decimal to an equivalent decimal with three decimal places to the right of the decimal point. One of the numbers shows a leading zero; also include this leading zero in all of the numbers:

0.016, 0.700, 0.203, 0.750

Now the decimals can be compared in the same manner as whole numbers, and 16 < 203 < 700 < 750, so the answer is .016, .203, 0.7, .75.

PRACTICE 1

Write the following numbers as decimals.

1. $3\frac{2}{10}$

2. $98\frac{3}{100}$

3. $23\frac{78}{1,000}$

4. 17 hundredths

5. 9 and 6 tenths

OPERATIONS AND DECIMALS

To add or subtract decimal values, line up the decimal points and add or subtract.

$$
\begin{array}{r}
12.87 \\
+\ 7.52 \\
\hline
20.39
\end{array}
$$

When you are multiplying decimals, first you multiply in the usual fashion, and then count over the proper number of places. This is done by counting how many places are to the right of the decimal points in each number you are multiplying.

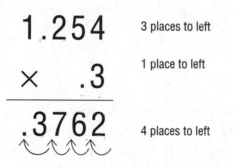

1.254   3 places to left

× .3   1 place to left

.3762   4 places to left

When you are dividing decimals, you move the decimal point of the dividend and divisor the same number of places.

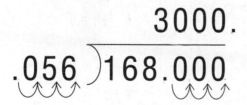

$$
.056\,)\overline{168.000}\quad = 3000.
$$

PRACTICE 2

1. $34.7 + 4.1 + 0.03 =$

2. $125.05 - 11.4 =$

3. $16.8 \times 0.2 =$

4. $5.34 \times 10 =$

5. $42.19 \times 0.4 =$

6. $1.95 \div 0.03 =$

7. $245 \div 4.9 =$

DECIMALS AND FRACTIONS

Decimals and fractions are two different ways to represent the same values. In other words, you can equate fractions and decimals. Let's look at the relationship between the fraction $\frac{1}{10}$ and the decimal 0.1. The following figure represents both values.

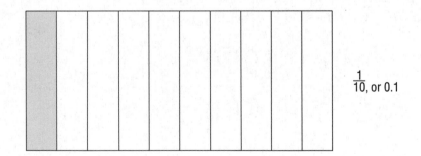

$\frac{1}{10}$, or 0.1

$\frac{1}{10}$ equals 0.1.

To convert a fraction to a decimal, just divide the top by the bottom. Look at the fraction $\frac{1}{2}$; $1 \div 2 = 0.5$, so $\frac{1}{2}$ is equal to 0.5.

TIP: In case you are asked to convert a fraction to a decimal, you should have some common conversions memorized.

Fraction	Decimal
$\frac{1}{2}$	0.5
$\frac{1}{3}$	$0.\overline{3}$
$\frac{2}{3}$	$0.\overline{6}$
$\frac{1}{4}$	0.25
$\frac{3}{4}$	0.75
$\frac{1}{5}$	0.2

PRACTICE 3

1. Convert $\frac{7}{8}$ to a decimal.

2. Convert 0.12 to a fraction.

3. Which is greatest?
0.4, 0.07, 0.25, 0.100, 0.009

4. Which is the smallest?
$\frac{4}{10}$, 0.5, 0.07, 0.0099, 0.071

5. Change $\frac{3}{4}$ to a decimal.

ANSWERS

Practice 1

1. 3.2
2. 98.03
3. 23.078
4. 0.17
5. 9.6

Practice 2

1. Add the numbers vertically; make sure to line up the decimal points and add trailing zeros when necessary:

$$\begin{array}{r} 34.70 \\ 4.10 \\ + \ 0.03 \\ \hline 38.83 \end{array}$$

2. When subtracting decimals, it is easiest to do the problem vertically, remembering to line up the decimal points.

$$\begin{array}{r} 125.05 \\ - \ 11.40 \\ \hline 113.65 \end{array}$$

3. Multiply without regard to the decimal points: $168 \times 2 = 336$. Because there are two digits to the right of the decimal points in the factors, move the decimal point two places left in the product: 3.36.

4. Use the shortcut when multiplying by 10. Move the decimal point one place to the right to get the product of 53.4.

5. Multiply without regard to the decimal point:

$$\begin{array}{r} 42.19 \\ \times \ 0.4 \\ \hline 16876 \end{array}$$

There are three digits to the right of the decimal points in the factors, namely 1, 9, and 4. Move the decimal point three places to the left: 16.876.

6. Set up the problem as a long division problem. The divisor (0.03) has two digits to the right of the decimal point, so you must move the decimal point two places to the right in both the divisor and the dividend (1.95). Then, move the decimal place straight up to the quotient to get an answer of 65.

7. Set up the problem as a long division problem. The divisor (4.9) has one digit to the right of the decimal point, so you must move the decimal place one place to the right in both the divisor and the dividend (245). You must add a trailing zero onto the dividend as a placeholder. Then move the decimal place straight up to the quotient to get 50.

Practice 3

1. $\frac{7}{8}$ means "seven divided by eight." Divide 7 by 8, using long division, to get 0.875.

2. 0.12 is read as "twelve hundredths." $\frac{12}{100} \div \frac{4}{4} = \frac{3}{25}$.

3. Change each decimal to an equivalent decimal—all of which have the same number of digits to the right of the decimal point: 0.4 = 0.400, 0.07 = 0.070, 0.25 = 0.250, 0.100, 0.009. Now 400 > 250 > 100 > 70 > 9; 0.4 is the greatest.

4. Change all numbers to decimals with four digits to the right of the decimal point: $\frac{2}{5} = \frac{4}{10}$, read as "four tenths." The decimal equivalent of $\frac{4}{10}$ = 0.4000. Also, 0.5 = 0.5000, 0.07 = 0.0700, 0.0099, 0.071 = 0.0710. Now, 5,000 > 4,000 > 710 > 700 > 99; 0.0099 is the smallest.

5. One of the common fractions that it is helpful to memorize the decimal equivalent of is 0.75. Also, $\frac{3}{4}$ is read as "three divided by four." Divide 3 by 4, using long division, to get 0.75.

6

ratios and proportions

A surprising proportion of mathematicians are accomplished
musicians. Is it because music and mathematics
share patterns that are beautiful?
—MARTIN GARDNER (1914–   )

You may have seen and have even worked with ratios and proportions in your daily life, whether in sports scores or maybe on a map of your state. This lesson will explain ratios and proportions and how to best work with them.

RATIOS ARE A way of comparing numbers, and they can be expressed in three ways. Suppose your school has five people with blonde hair for every seven people with brown hair. This information, expressed as a ratio, would be as follows:

1. as a sentence:

There is a five-to-seven ratio of blondes to brunettes.

2. using a colon:

5:7

3. using a bar:

$\frac{5}{7}$

Like fractions, ratios can be reduced to smaller terms. A person may count that your class has 10 blondes and 14 brunettes and state that there is a 10-to-14 ratio. This is accurate because $\frac{10}{14}$ reduces to $\frac{5}{7}$.

SCALE DRAWINGS

Sometimes, you will encounter ratio questions that deal with scale drawings. **Scale drawings** are used to represent objects that are too large or too small to be drawn or built to actual size. The scale is determined by the ratio of a given length on the drawing or model to its corresponding length in real life.

How does this work? Suppose you are given a map with a scale of 1 inch = 90 miles. If the distance between Virginia Beach, Virginia, and New York City, New York, on the map is 4 inches, what is the actual distance?

The ratio is $\frac{1 \text{ inch}}{90 \text{ miles}}$. Set that equal to $\frac{4 \text{ inches}}{x}$ and cross multiply:

$$1x = (90)(4)$$
$$x = 360$$

So, the actual distance is 360 miles.

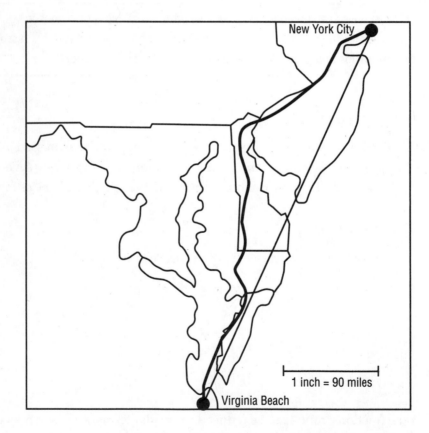

PROPORTIONS

A **proportion** is an equation that shows that two ratios are equivalent. Usually, proportions are written using ratios with bars.

When written as $a{:}b = c{:}d$, a and d are the **extremes** (they are on the **end**), and b and c are the **means** (they are in the **middle**). The product of the means equals the product of the extremes.

When written as a fraction, the **cross products** are equal. This is useful in determining whether two fractions are a proportion. Try one. Are $\frac{9}{12}$ and $\frac{18}{24}$ a proportion? Multiply the cross products to see:

$24 \times 9 = 18 \times 12$?

$216 = 216$; these fractions represent a proportion.

Proportions can be used to convert units. Look at the following conversions:

1 foot = 12 inches

3 feet = 1 yard

1 mile = 5,280 feet   *1,760 yds*

1 minute = 60 seconds

1 hour = 60 minutes

1 meter = 10 decimeters

1 cup = 8 ounces

1 pint = 2 cups

1 quart = 2 pints

1 gallon = 4 quarts

1 meter = 100 centimeters

1 meter = 1,000 millimeters

If you know that 1 minute equals 60 seconds, you can easily figure out how many minutes are in 300 seconds by setting up a proportion:

$$\frac{1 \text{ minute}}{60 \text{ seconds}} = \frac{?\text{ minutes}}{300 \text{ seconds}}$$

When you use the fraction form of proportions, you can cross multiply to solve for any unknown. Cross multiplying, you get $1 \times 300 = 60 \times ?$, or $300 = 60 \times ?$. Dividing both sides by 60, you get $? = 5$.

TIP: You should always convert your units *before* you set up a proportion. Suppose you knew that 12 inches of fabric costs $0.60, and you needed to order 20 feet of it to design an outfit. First, you would convert the 20 feet into inches. You know 1 foot equals 12 inches, so you need to multiply:

$$20 \text{ feet} \times \frac{12 \text{ inches}}{1 \text{ foot}} = 240 \text{ inches}$$

To find the price for 240 inches, set up a proportion:

$$\frac{12 \text{ inches}}{\$0.60} = \frac{240 \text{ inches}}{\$?}$$

$$12 \times ? = (0.60)(240)$$

$$12 \times ? = 144$$

$$? = \frac{144}{12} = \$12$$

DIRECT AND INVERSE PROPORTIONS

If two proportions are **directly proportional**, then one increases by a certain factor as the other increases by the same factor. If one decreases by a certain factor, the other decreases by that same factor.

If you have an after-school or weekend job, the amount of money you earn may be directly proportional to the amount of hours that you work. Maybe if you work twice as long, you make twice as much. If you work half the amount you usually work in one week, you earn half the money you usually get.

Two proportions are **inversely proportional** if an increase by a certain factor for one is accompanied by a decrease by that same factor for the other.

PRACTICE

1. On the beach, the ratio of boogie boards to surf boards is 12 to 3. If there are 84 boogie boards, how many surf boards are there on the beach?

2. There are 48 people on a camping trip. Sixteen are female. What is the ratio of male to female?

3. Two numbers are in the ratio of 5 to 8. If the larger number is 72, what is the smaller number?

4. A set of dollhouse furniture is made to scale and is $\frac{1}{72}$ the size of real furniture; it has a scale of 1 to 72. If a real table is 6 feet in length, what is the length of the corresponding dollhouse table?

5. Strawberries are 3 quarts for $4.98. How much will 10 quarts of strawberries cost?

ANSWERS

1. Set up a proportion based on the ratio $\frac{\text{boogie boards}}{\text{surf boards}}$:
$$\frac{12}{3} = \frac{84}{x}$$
$$3 \times 84 = 12 \times x$$
Cross multiply: $252 = 12 \times x$. Now, divide by 12: $21 = x$. There are 21 surf boards.

2. You are given the total number of people and the number of females. The question is, what is the ratio of male to female? There are $48 - 16 = 32$ males on the trip. The ratio of male to female is $\frac{\text{male}}{\text{female}} = \frac{32}{16} = \frac{2}{1}$. The ratio of male to female is 2 to 1.

3. Set up a proportion based on the ratio $\frac{\text{smaller number}}{\text{larger number}}$.
$$\frac{5}{8} = \frac{n}{72}$$
$$8 \times n = 5 \times 72$$
Now, cross multiply: $8 \times n = 360$. Divide by 8: $n = 45$. The smaller number is 45.

4. The ratio of dollhouse to real is 1 to 72. The problem states that the real table is 6 feet in length. Knowing that the dollhouse table will be much smaller, first convert 6 feet to 72 inches. Because the ratio is 1 to 72, and the real table is 72 inches, the dollhouse table is 1 inch.

5. Set up a proportion of $\frac{\text{quarts of strawberries}}{\text{price}}$.
$$\frac{3}{4.98} = \frac{10}{p}$$
$$4.98 \times 10 = 3 \times p$$
Cross multiply: $49.8 = 3 \times p$. Now, divide by 3: $16.6 = p$. The price is $16.60.

percents

We use only 10% of our brains. Imagine how smart
we would be if we used the other 60%!
—ELLEN DEGENERES (1958–)

This lesson will examine the basics of percents and their relationships with fractions and decimals. Learn how to find percent values in equations and word problems.

MOST LIKELY, YOU have encountered the percent (%) symbol sometime during your life—maybe when receiving a test score or even looking through a store's sales flyer. When you see a number followed by the percent symbol, you can think of the percent as a ratio comparing that number to 100.

$25\% = \frac{25}{100}$

$50\% = \frac{50}{100}$

$75\% = \frac{75}{100}$

Percents can be expressed in two different ways:

1. as a fraction (just put the number over 100): $5\% = \frac{5}{100}$

2. as a decimal (move the decimal point two places to the left): $5\% = 0.05$

TIP: Get familiar with some common fraction and decimal equivalents to percents.

Percent	Fraction	Decimal
25%	$\frac{1}{4}$	0.25
50%	$\frac{1}{2}$	0.50
75%	$\frac{3}{4}$	0.75
100%	$\frac{1}{1}$	1

PRACTICE 1

Fill in the following chart with the decimal and fraction equivalent to the given percent. More than one response may be correct. The first has been completed for you as a guide.

When I See . . .	I Will Write . . .
25%	$\frac{1}{4}$ and 0.25
32%	
80%	
95%	
150%	
500%	

FINDING THE PERCENT OF A NUMBER

Recall that the word *of* tells you to multiply. When you take the percent *of* a number, you should multiply.

Suppose you are purchasing a graphic novel that usually costs $8, but the comic book store is selling it for 25% off. How much do you take off of $8?

Remember that $25\% = \frac{25}{100}$, or $\frac{1}{4}$, so you are taking off $\frac{1}{4}$ of $8; $\frac{1}{4}$ of $8 translates to $\frac{1}{4} \times 8$, which equals $2 off. So, the graphic novel is yours for the price of $6!

What if you are asked to find the percent of a percent of a number? Don't panic just yet! When you take the percent of a percent, all you need to do is multiply. Let's try one:

40% of 20% of 600 =

0.40 of 0.20 of 600 =

$0.40 \times 0.20 \times 600 = 48$

INTO THE UNKNOWN

When you see the phrase *seven percent*, you know to express this mathematically as $\frac{7}{100}$. What about when you see the phrase *what percent*? How do you express this mathematically? If you're thinking, "I don't know," then you're right. That's right—when you are asked *what percent*, you are being asked to determine an unknown value.

Instead of writing "I don't know" in the place of the numbers that you don't know, try using a variable, such as x.

TIP: A **variable** is a letter used to represent a number value. (For more information on variables, see Lesson 10.)

Let's put this into practice. What percent of 250 is 30?

What percent means $\frac{x}{100}$

of 250 means $\cdot\ 250$

is 30 means $= 30$

$\frac{x}{100} \cdot 250 = 30$

$x \cdot \frac{250}{100} = 30$

$x \cdot 250 = 30 \cdot 100$

$x \cdot 250 = 3{,}000$

$x = 12$

PERCENT ESTIMATION

Sometimes, it may be quicker for you to estimate a percent value. What if you were asked to estimate 19% of 50?

Use 20% as a "friendlier" percent: 20% of 50 = 10, so 19% of 50 is about 10.

PERCENT OF CHANGE

To find a percent increase or decrease, first find the amount of increase or decrease. Then, use the percent of change formula:

$$\text{amount change} = \frac{x}{100} \times \text{original number}$$

Let's put this into play. Find the percent decrease from 4 to 3.

First, determine what the actual decrease is. The decrease from 4 to 3 is 1. Now, plug the information you know into the percent of change formula:

$$1 = \frac{x}{100} \cdot 4$$

Now, solve for *x*:

$$1 = \frac{4x}{100}$$
$$1 = \frac{x}{25}$$
$$25 = x$$

So, the percent decrease from 4 to 3 is 25%.

PURCHASING AND PERCENTS

Some percent questions involve buying or selling items. A **discount** is the amount by which the regular price of an item is reduced. A **markup** is the difference between the price paid by the seller and the increased selling price, which is the amount you pay for the item.

Let's look at a discount question.

A book on your summer reading list originally cost $15, but during a summer sale, it's being sold at a 15% discount.

First, find 15% of $15:

$$\left(\tfrac{15}{100}\right)(15) = \$2.25$$

So, the discount is $2.25. Now subtract $2.25 from the original price of $15:

$$\begin{array}{r} \$15.00 \\ -\ 2.25 \\ \hline \$12.75 \end{array}$$

During the sale, you can get the book for $12.75!

Now, on the other side, let's try a markup question.

A local sporting goods store paid $1,300 for a mountain bike. The store has marked the bike up by 30%.

First, find 30% of $1,300:

$$\left(\tfrac{30}{100}\right)(1,300) = \$390$$

Now, add this $390 markup to the original price:

$$\begin{array}{r} \$1,300 \\ +\ 390 \\ \hline \$1,690 \end{array}$$

The store is selling the mountain bike for $1,690.

PRACTICE 2

1. What is 57% of 350?

2. What percent of 200 is 68?

3. Nineteen is 76% of what number?

4. Two out of every five members of the after-school club are male. What percentage of the after-school club is male?

5. Hockey sticks that normally sell for $89 are on sale for 35% off the regular price. There is also a 6% sales tax. How much will the stick cost after the sale and the sales tax?

6. The book club attendance rose from 25 members to 30 members. What is the percent increase in membership, to the nearest percent?

7. Out of the 28 selections on the menu, four of them are desserts. What percentage, to the nearest tenth, of the menu are NOT desserts?

ANSWERS

Practice 1

When I See . . .	I Will Write . . .
25%	$\frac{1}{4}$ and 0.25
32%	0.32, $\frac{32}{100}$, $\frac{8}{25}$
80%	$\frac{80}{100}$, $\frac{4}{5}$, 0.8
95%	$\frac{95}{100}$, $\frac{19}{20}$, 0.95
150%	$\frac{150}{100}$, $\frac{3}{2}$, 1.5
500%	$\frac{500}{100}$, 5

Practice 2

1. One method of solution is to set up a proportion: $\frac{\text{part}}{\text{whole}} = \frac{\text{percent}}{100}$. The "whole" is 350, and the "part" is what is being requested in the problem. Substitute the given information: $\frac{n}{350} = \frac{57}{100}$. Cross multiply to get $350 \times 57 = n \times 100$, and then multiply 350 times 57: $19,950 = n \times 100$. Divide 19,950 by 100 to get 199.50 or the equivalent 199.5.

2. Set up an equation. Remember that *of* means multiply and *is* means equals. Make a straight translation using the variable p for percent: $p \times 200 = 68$. Divide 68 by 200 to get 0.34. This is the answer as a decimal. Change this answer to a percent by multiplying by 100 to get 34%.

3. Set up a proportion: $\frac{19}{n} = \frac{76}{100}$. In the problem, 19 is the "part," 76 is the percent, and the "whole" is what you need to calculate. Cross multiply to get $n \times 76 = 19 \times 100$. Multiply: $n \times 76 = 1,900$. Now divide 1,900 by 76 to get 25.

4. Two out of every five points to a ratio, so use the proportion: $\frac{2}{5} = \frac{p}{100}$. Cross multiply to get $5 \times p = 2 \times 100$. Multiply: $5 \times p = 200$. Now, divide 200 by 5 to get 40%.

5. This is a multistep problem, because the sale percentage is a percent decrease, and the sales tax is a percent increase. There are several methods to solve this problem. The key word *is* means equals, *of* means multiply, and 35% is 0.35 written as a decimal. Set up the equation: discount = percent × original, or $d = 0.35 \times 89$. Multiply to get the discount, which is $31.15. The sale price is $89 − $31.15 = $57.85. The sales tax is then calculated based on this sale price: sales tax = percent × sale price. The tax will be $t = 0.06 \times \$57.85$, or $t = \$3.47$, rounded to the nearest cent. Add this to the sales price to find the cost of the stick: $57.85 + $3.47 = $61.32.

6. This is a percent increase problem, so set up the proportion: $\frac{\text{change}}{\text{original}} = \frac{\text{percent}}{100}$. The change in attendance is $30 - 25 = 5$. The original attendance is 25 members. The proportion setup is $\frac{5}{25} = \frac{p}{100}$. Cross multiply to get $25 \times p = 5 \times 100$. Multiply 5 times 100 to get $25 \times p = 500$. Divide 500 by 25, and the percent is therefore 20%.

7. The problem asks what percentage are NOT desserts. Because four of the 28 selections are desserts, then $28 - 4 = 24$ selections are NOT desserts. Set up the proportion: $\frac{24}{28} = \frac{p}{100}$. Cross multiply: $28 \times p = 24 \times 100$, or $28 \times p = 2,400$. Divide 2,400 by 28 to get the percent, rounded to the nearest tenth, or 85.7%.

measures of central tendency

Measure what is measurable, and
make measurable what is not so.
—GALILEO GALILEI (1564–1642)

This lesson will explore the basic measures of central tendency—mean, median, mode, and range.

WHEN YOU ARE dealing with sets of numbers, there are measures used to describe the set as a whole. These are called **measures of central tendency**, and they include mean, median, mode, and range.

Mean is another way of saying average. To find the average, you total up all the values and then divide by the number of values.

$$\text{mean} = \frac{\text{total of all values}}{\text{number of values}}$$

Sound easy enough? Let's try a problem:

Find the mean of the following set: {17, 22, 18, 31, 27, 17}

Add up the six numbers in the set: $17 + 22 + 18 + 31 + 27 + 17 = 132$.

Now, divide 132 by 6, the number of entries in the set: $132 \div 6 = 22$.

The mean (or average) of the set is 22.

Let's try another.

> The temperature, in degrees Fahrenheit, for the first week of July is as follows: 84, 88, 86, 87, 80, 84, and 86. What is the average temperature for the week?
>
> Add up the seven temperatures: 84 + 88 + 86 + 87 + 80 + 84 + 86 = 595; 595 divided by 7, the number of days measured, is 595 ÷ 7 = 85. The average temperature is 85° Fahrenheit.

....

TIP: If you are asked to find the mean of a set of numbers, and the set is evenly spaced apart such as 2, 4, 6, 8, 10, 12, 14, the mean is the middle number in this set, because there is an odd number of data items. In this example, the mean is 8. If there is an even number of data items, there are two middle numbers: 4, 8, 12, 16, 20, and 24. In this case, the mean is the average of the two middle numbers: 12 + 16 = 28, and 28 divided by 2 is 14.

....

When you are considering a list of values in order (from smallest to largest), the **median** is the middle value. If there are two "middle" values, then you just take their average.

Let's find the median of 2, 8, 3, 4, 7, 6, and 6. First you put these numbers in order:

2 3 4 6 6 7 8

Next, circle the middle number:

2 3 4 ⑥ 6 7 8

What's the median of the following?

2 3 4 4 6 6 7 8

The numbers are already listed in order, so you don't have to worry about arranging them. Notice that this list of numbers has two middle terms:

2 3 4 **4 6** 6 7 8

In this case, you need to take the average of these two numbers to find the median.

$$4 + 6 = \frac{10}{2} = 5$$

The median is 5.

In a list of values, the **mode** is the number that occurs the most. If two numbers occur "the most," then you have two modes. This is called **bimodal**.

Let's find the mode of the following numbers:

35 52 17 23 51 52 18 32

In this series of numbers, you see that 52 appears twice.

35 **52** 17 23 51 **52** 18 32

So, the mode is 52.

The **range** indicates how close together the given values are to one another in a set of data. To find the range, determine the difference between the largest and the smallest values in the set of data. Subtract the smallest value from the largest value in the set.

Let's see how this works.

Find the ranges of ages in the community play, given these ages in years: 68, 54, 49, 40, 39, 39, 24, 22, 20, 10, and 10.

The range of ages is 68 − 10 = 58 years.

Now, find the range of this set: {42, 40, 45, 43, 43, 40, 45}

Find the largest and smallest values in the set. In this example, these are 45 and 40, respectively. The difference between 45 and 40, the range, is 45 − 40 = 5.

PRACTICE 1

1. Find the mean of the following set of data: {32, 34, 34, 35, 37, 38, 34, 42}

2. What is the mode of {71, 68, 71, 77, 65, 68, 72}?

3. The ages at the day camp were as follows: 9, 12, 9, 10, 9, 13, 11, 8, 17, 10. What is the median age?

4. What is the range of the temperatures listed: 43°, 47°, 43°, 52°, 42°, 78°, 84°, 80°?

ANSWERS

1. To find the mean, add up all of the data values, and divide by the number of items, which is eight: 32 + 34 + 34 + 35 + 37 + 38 + 34 + 42 = 286; 286 divided by 8 is 35.75.

2. There are two modes for this data set. Both 71 and 68 appear in the set twice.

3. First, arrange the data into increasing order: 8, 9, 9, 9, 10, 10, 11, 12, 13, 17. There is an even number of data values, so the median is the mean of the two middle values. The middle values are 10 + 10 = 20, and 20 divided by 2 is 10.

4. The range is the difference between the highest and lowest values in the set of data. The highest temperature is 84° and the lowest temperature is 42°: 84° − 42° = 42°.

9

graphs that display data

Errors using inadequate data are
much less than using no data at all.
CHARLES BABBAGE (1792–1871)

In this lesson, you will be visually introduced to the many graphs used to display data, including tables, bar graphs, line graphs, scatter plots, pie charts, pictographs, and stem-and-leaf plots.

GRAPHS ARE INCREDIBLY useful because they communicate information visually. You probably have read graphs in newspapers, magazines, online, or in the classroom. When complicated information is difficult to understand, an illustration—or graph—can help get your point across quickly.

Tables are used to organize information into columns and rows. Usually, a title of the data presented is located at the top of the table, and there may be descriptions or titles in the column heads or row heads. Before looking at the data, you should ask yourself "What is this table telling me?" By focusing on what the table tells you, you will be able to find the data that you need easier, and analyze it.

×	0	1	2	3	4	5	6	7	8	9	10	11	12
0	0	0	0	0	0	0	0	0	0	0	0	0	0
1	0	1	2	3	4	5	6	7	8	9	10	11	12
2	0	2	4	6	8	10	12	14	16	18	20	22	24
3	0	3	6	9	12	15	18	21	24	27	30	33	36
4	0	4	8	12	16	20	24	28	32	36	40	44	48
5	0	5	10	15	20	25	30	35	40	45	50	55	60
6	0	6	12	18	24	30	36	42	48	54	60	66	72
7	0	7	14	21	28	35	42	49	56	63	70	77	84
8	0	8	16	24	32	40	48	56	64	72	80	88	96
9	0	9	18	27	36	45	54	63	72	81	90	99	108
10	0	10	20	30	40	50	60	70	80	90	100	110	120
11	0	11	22	33	44	55	66	77	88	99	110	121	132
12	0	12	24	36	48	60	72	84	96	108	120	132	144

PRACTICE 1

Use this table to answer the following question.

Scoops	Number of free toppings
1	2
2	5
3	7
4	10
5	12
6	
7	
8	
9	

On Wednesday, at the ice cream parlor where Amy works, there's a special on free toppings.

If Ms. Taylor receives 17 free toppings with the ice cream she buys, how many scoops of ice cream did she buy?

Bar graphs are easy to read and understand. Bar graphs can be used to present one type of data, or may contain different colored bars that allow for a side-by-side comparison of similar statistics.

When you read a bar graph, there are several things you must pay attention to—the title, two axes, and the bars.

The title gives an overview of the information being presented in the bar graph. The title is usually given at the top of the graph.

Each bar graph has two axes, which are labeled. The axes labels inform you what information is presented on each axis. One axis represents data groups; the other represents the frequency of the data groups.

The bars are rectangular blocks that can have their base at either the vertical axis or the horizontal axis. Each bar represents the data for one of the data groups.

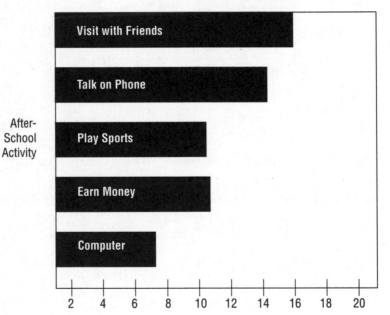

PRACTICE 2

Use the bar graph to answer the following questions.

South Orange School interviewed its students over seven years to compare how many students owned dogs to cats.

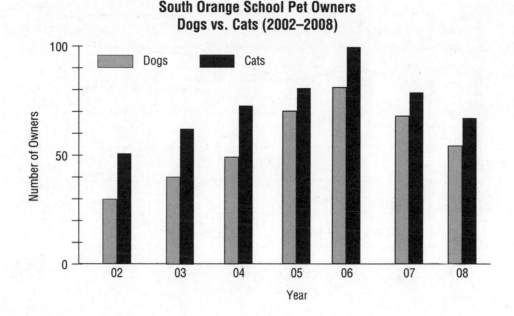

1. What is the name of the bar graph?

2. Every year displayed on the bar graph shows that more people owned

   _____.

3. In 2002, how many people owned dogs?

4. In what year did 100 people own cats?

5. How many more people owned cats than dogs in 2005?

Line graphs aren't as pretty to look at as bar graphs, but they are easy to read. Again, different types of data may be presented at the same time, as in the following case.

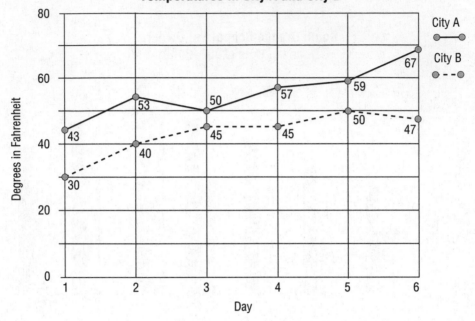

It may help you to think of a line graph as being formed by connecting the topmost points of vertical bars on a bar graph and then erasing the bars.

Line graphs are good to display information that continues, such as temperatures or snowfall.

PRACTICE 3

Use the following line graph to answer questions 1–4.

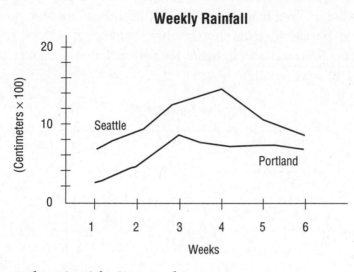

1. What is the title of the line graph?

2. What is the difference between rainfall in Portland and in Seattle in Week 3?

3. For which week is the difference in rainfall the least?

4. For which week is the difference the greatest?

    Scatter plots have points scattered all over the place.

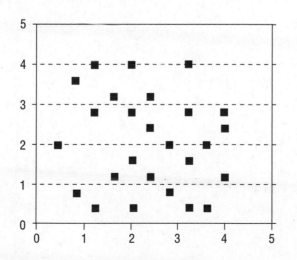

Like line graphs, scatter plots use horizontal and vertical axes to plot data points. However, scatter plots show how much one variable is affected by another.

Scatter plots usually consist of a large body of data. The closer the data points come when plotted to making a straight line, the higher the connection between the two variables, or the stronger the relationship.

If the data points make a straight line rising from left to right, then the variables have a positive correlation.

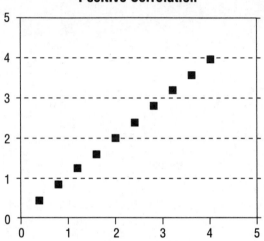

Positive Correlation

If the line goes from a high value on the left down to a right axis, the variables have a negative correlation.

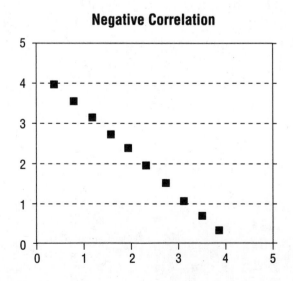

Negative Correlation

Pie charts, or circle graphs, are a great way to "see" data. Pie charts represent a whole, or 100%, as shown in this one.

Favorite Extreme Sports of Eighth Graders

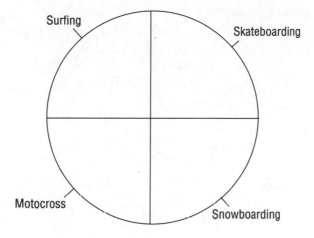

You can make some rough estimations regarding the different slices of the pie just by glancing at the chart. For example, if a slice is about a quarter of the pie, you can say "Hey, that's about 25%." Sometimes these charts are two-dimensional, and sometimes they are three-dimensional. As always, you should approach a chart wondering "What is this chart telling me?"

PRACTICE 4

Use the next pie chart to answer the following questions.

Bill's BBQ Joint uses various techniques to tell people about their world-famous ribs. Following is a pie chart showing how they break down every dollar used for advertising.

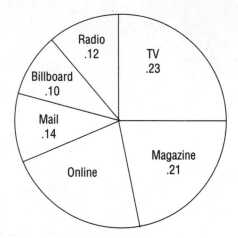

Bill's BBQ Joint Advertising Budget

1. What percent of Bill's BBQ Joint advertising dollar is spent on radio and TV?

2. How many cents of each dollar does Bill's BBQ Joint spend on online advertising?

3. On which advertising technique does Bill's BBQ Joint spend the most?

Instead of using lines, bars, or chunks of pie to represent data, **pictographs** use pictures. You may see these types of graphs in newspapers and magazines.

Pictographs are also sometimes called **picture graphs** or **histograms**. Each picture on a pictograph represents a quantity of something. There is a key to tell you what each picture means. Here is an example of a pictograph.

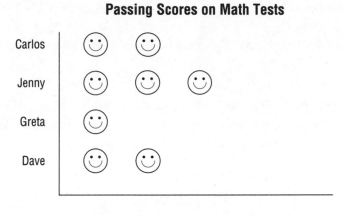

Passing Scores on Math Tests

Key: ☺ represents a month of 70%+ scores

PRACTICE 5

Use the next pictogram to answer the following questions.

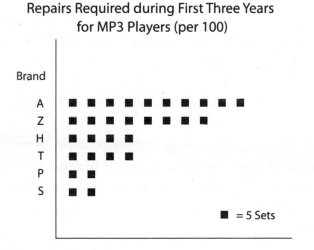

Repairs Required during First Three Years
for MP3 Players (per 100)

■ = 5 Sets

1. What is the name of this pictogram?

2. What does each symbol represent?

3. How many more Brand A MP3 players per hundred needed repairs during the first three years than Brand T MP3 players per hundred?

4. What percent of Brand Z MP3 players needed repairs during the first three years?

5. How many more Brand Z MP3 players were sold than Brand P during the three years?

Stem-and-leaf plots are the least understandable of all the charts you have studied so far. In other words, if you never saw a stem-and-leaf plot before, it is hard to tell what one means. Look at the graphic.

Stem	Leaf
2	1 4 6
3	2 5 7
4	3 8 9
5	1 2 4
6	3 5 7

A stem-and-leaf plot splits number data into a "stem" and a "leaf." The leaf is the last digits of the number and the other digits to the left of the leaf form the stem. The number 149 would be split as:

stem   leaf

1   4 9

As you can see, the original value—149—can still be found.

Like scatter plots and pictographs, stem-and-leaf plots show the frequency with which certain things occur.

PRACTICE 6

Show the following values on a stem-and-leaf plot.

12, 13, 21, 27, 33, 34, 35, 37, 40, 40, 41

ANSWERS

Practice 1

Look for the pattern in the free toppings. The difference between 2 and 5 is 3. The difference between 5 and 7 is 2. So, the pattern is 3, 2, 3, 2. That means that the next number of free toppings (for 6 scoops) would be 12 + 3, or 15, and the next (7 scoops) would be 15 + 2, or 17.

Practice 2

1. South Orange School Pet Owners for Dogs vs. Cats (2002–2008)
2. cats
3. 30
4. 2006
5. 10

Practice 3

1. Weekly Rainfall
2. Go to the Week 3 mark. There were 12 inches of rainfall for Seattle—each mark is two from the last. Multiply 12 by 100, because the axes label tells you that each mark is centimeters × 100: 12 × 100 = 1,200. There were 8 inches of rainfall for Portland—each mark is two from the last. Multiply by 100: 8 × 100 = 800. Now, subtract to find the difference: 1,200 − 800 = 400 centimeters.
3. The lines are closest together at Week 6.
4. The lines are farthest apart at Week 4.

Practice 4

1. 35%. Bill's BBQ Joint spends 35 cents, which is 35% of the total dollar.
2. 20 cents. Remember, a pie chart represents 100%, in this case a dollar, or 100 cents. Add up all the given amounts to find how much was spent on all advertising, except online: .21 + .23 + .12 + .10 + .14 = .80. That leaves 20 cents.
3. Television. Bill's BBQ Joint must love the camera because they spend .23 of every dollar on TV advertising.

Practice 5

1. Repairs Required during First Three Years for MP3 Players (per 100)
2. Five MP3 players
3. The key tells you that each symbol represents five MP3 players. The row for Brand A contains six more symbols than the row for Brand T. Multiply 6 by 5 to get 30 more sets per hundred.
4. Percent is a fraction of 100. This pictograph displays repairs per hundred MP3 players sold, so it actually shows percents and each symbol represents 5%. Brand Z has eight symbols in its row. So, $8 \times 5\% = 40\%$. This is the percent of repairs on Brand Z during the first three years.
5. Be careful! This is a trick question. The pictograph contains no information about sales, so there is not enough information to answer this question.

Practice 6

Stem	Leaf
1	2 3
2	1 7
3	3 4 5 7
4	0 0 1

SECTION 2

basic algebra—
the mysteries of letters,
numbers, and symbols

IN THE NINTH century, an Arabic author named al'Khwarizmi wrote a math treatise. His writing, called *Hisab al-jabr w'al-muqabala*, introduced the term *al-jabr*, which eventually evolved into the word and math process we know today as algebra.

In al'Khwarizmi's time, *al-jabr* meant the "reunion of broken parts." This is how you can think of algebra. The broken parts—letters, numbers, symbols—come together to form a whole algebraic statement. And by learning the language, you will be able to easily translate these statements and to "speak" algebra clearly.

Algebraic concepts are nothing new. They can be found in the relics of ancient Egypt and Babylon, and later throughout early Europe and Asia. But now, thousands of years later, algebra is still proving to be a subject that many people need help with. This section will introduce you to the basic concepts of algebra, including:

- variables
- expressions
- equations
- inequalities
- powers and exponents
- scientific notation
- square roots
- algebraic word problems

variables, expressions, and equations

Algebra is, properly speaking, the analysis of equations.
—JOSEPH ALFRED SERRET (1819–1885)

This lesson will break down the basic algebra group of variables, expressions, and equations.

ALGEBRA IS A type of math that uses variables to represent values. If numbers were secret agents, variables would be the disguises they wear. In algebra, you can use a letter to represent a number. And if you come across a variable, you can find its real identity by using any clues you find. In algebra, letters, called **variables**, are often used to stand in for numbers. Variables are usually written in italics. The z in $z + 21 = 8$ is a variable.

Any letter can be used to represent a number in an algebraic expression. The letters x, y, and z are commonly used.

Variables can represent any quantity—an integer, a decimal, or even a fraction. A variable can also represent a positive or a negative number.

Once you realize that these variables are really numbers incognito, you'll see that they follow all the rules of mathematics, just like numbers do. This can help you figure out what number the variable you're focusing on stands for.

A **term** is a number or a number and the variable(s) associated with it. For example:

7

$6b$

$15xy$

When a number is placed next to a variable, the number is the **coefficient** of the variable. When you are multiplying a number and a variable, you just have to write them side by side. You don't need to use a multiplication symbol. Let's see a few examples.

$8c$ 8 is the coefficient of the variable c.

$6ab$ 6 is the coefficient of both variables, a and b.

If two or more terms have exactly the same variable, they are said to be **like terms**. Look at these examples:

$7x + 3x$

$45d - 31d$

When you combine $12x$ and $14x$ into $26x$, you are **combining like terms**. What does this mean? Here, $12x$ and $14x$ are considered **like terms** because they both involve the variable x. The numbers 3 and the 4 are called coefficients of the x term. For the previous examples,

$7x + 3x = 10x$

$45d - 31d = 14d$

TIP: A term with no coefficient actually has a coefficient of one: $y = 1y$.

Combine like terms carefully—check to make sure that the variables are exactly the same!

EXPRESSIONS

An **expression** is a mathematical statement that can use numbers, variables, or a combination of the two. Sometimes, there are operations, but there is *never* an equal sign. Expressions include

8

$8x$

$8x + 9$

$8x + 9 \div 2y$

Notice that the value of an expression changes as the value of the variable changes. Let's see how this works:

If $x = 1$, then $x + 6 = 1 + 6 = 7$

If $x = 2$, then $x + 6 = 2 + 6 = 8$

If $x = 3$, then $x + 6 = 3 + 6 = 9$

If $x = 100$, then $x + 6 = 100 + 6 = 106$

If $x = 213$, then $x + 6 = 213 + 6 = 219$

If you are given a phrase, you can turn it into an expression by looking for operations, variables, and numbers. Suppose you were asked for the math expression equal to *the quotient of three divided by a number plus the difference between three and two.*

The word *quotient* means to divide, so you write "$3 \div$." The word *number* represents your variable, so use the variable x: $3 \div x$. The word *plus* means to add, so now you have "$3 \div x +$." Finally, the word *difference* means to subtract, so the final expression will be $3 \div x + (3 - 2)$.

Sometimes, you will be able to simplify expressions (especially if there are any like terms). In order to simplify expressions, there are several things you have to know. When simplifying expressions, you should start by working inside the parentheses. Let's take a closer look:

$$(3x + 4y - 7) - (5x - 3y - 7)$$

Start inside the parentheses. If you'd like, you can change any subtract to "plus the opposite." For example, you could change $(5x - 3y - 7)$ to $(5x + -3y + -7)$. Some people think that addition is easier to work with when you are combining like terms:

$$3x + 4y + -7 + -5x + 3y + 7$$

Now, combine all the like terms, xs, and ys:

$$-2x + 7y$$

TIP: When you simplify expressions, don't forget the order of operations from Lesson 2:

P	Do operations inside *Parentheses*.
E	Evaluate terms with *Exponents*. (You will learn more about exponents in Lesson 13.)
M D	Do *Multiplication* and *Division* in order from left to right.
A S	*Add* and *Subtract* terms in order from left to right.

Expressions have known values *only* when you know the values of the variables. To find the value of an expression, plug in the known values of its variables. This is called **evaluating** an expression. Try to evaluate $25 \div (x + y)$, when $x = 2$ and $y = 3$.

Plug the known numbers into the expression:

$$25 \div (2 + 3)$$

Now, just use the order operations to solve this expression:

$$25 \div (5)$$
$$25 \div 5 = 5$$

EQUATIONS

An **equation** helps people solve many real-life problems. The word *equation* means two equal expressions. These expressions could be numbers such as $6 = 5 + 1$ or variables such as $d = rt$. In other words, an equation is a mathematical statement that can use numbers, variables, or a combination of the two *and* an equal sign. Examples include

$$8 = 8$$
$$8x = 16$$
$$8x + 9 = 26$$
$$8x + 9 \div 2y = 13$$

Let's practice writing a few expressions and equations.

five less than a number	$x-5$
a number increased by 12	$x+12$
twice a number decreased by 5	$2x-5$
the quotient of a number divided by three	$\frac{x}{3}$
three times the sum of a number and 13	$3(x+13)$
seven less than a number equals ten	$x-7=10$
a number increased by 17 equals 49	$x+17=49$
twice a number decreased by fifteen equals two	$2x-15=2$
the quotient of a number and six equals twelve	$\frac{x}{6}=12$

TIP: Questions that involve addition will use words like *plus, sum, more than, increased by, total, in all.*

Questions that involve subtraction will use words like *minus, difference, less than, fewer than, subtract, decreased by.*

Multiplication questions will contain words like *times, product, multiplied, each, of.*

Words that indicate a division question will contain words like *dividend, quotient, separated.*

You will often have to form equations out of words: "48 is 8 more than a number" can be translated to $48 = x + 8$; "15 times a number is 45" can be written as $15x = 45$.

TIP: Think of an expression as a phrase or series of words without a verb. Take, for example, $29b + 23$ or $m - 31$. A verb, which would be an equality or inequality symbol, would give value to the statement, turning it into an equation or inequality. These symbols include $=$, $\neq$, $>$, $<$, $\leq$, and $\geq$.

PRACTICE

Change the given information into an equation or expression as indicated.

1. You and your best friend have 167 buddies on your MySpace pages. Write an equation using variables to represent the number of friends you have and the number of friends your best friend has.

2. You are shopping for two new video games that have different prices. Use a variable to represent the cost of the first video game and a different variable to represent the cost of the second video game. Write an expression for these variables.

3. Your relatives have given you three gift cards to Pizza Palace as a reward for passing a difficult math test. Each gift card is for a different amount. The total amount you have to spend is $28. Set up an equation showing this information.

Find the expression, using the variable k for the number.

4. three more than a number

5. twice the sum of a number and three

6. three more than twice a number

7. three more than half a number

8. half of four times a number

Find the equation, using the variable f for the number.

9. seven more than a number equals twenty-one

10. four times the sum of a number and two equals forty-eight

11. six more than twice a number equals seventy

12. three more than one-third a number equals sixteen

Evaluate the following expression using the numbers given.

$x + 2x + 10$

13. when $x = 1$

14. when $x = -1$

15. when $x = 5$

ANSWERS

1. Your variables may be different, but your equation will look something like this: $m + f = 167$
2. Your variables may be different, but your expression will look something like this: $v + w$
3. Your variables may be different, but your equation will look something like this: $q + r + s = \$28$
4. $3 + k$
5. $2(k + 3)$
6. $3 + 2k$
7. $3 + \frac{1}{2}k$
8. $\frac{1}{2}(4k)$
9. $7 + f = 21$
10. $4(f + 2) = 48$
11. $6 + 2f = 70$
12. $3 + \frac{1}{3}f = 16$
    $x + 2x + 10$
13. Substitute 1 for x: $1 + 2(1) + 10 = 1 + 2 + 10 = 13$
14. Substitute -1 for x: $-1 + 2(-1) + 10 = -1 + -2 + 10 = -3 + 10 = 7$
15. Substitute 5 for x: $5 + 2(5) + 10 = 5 + 10 + 10 = 25$

solving equations

A problem well stated is half-solved.
—JOHN DEWEY (1859–1952)

Now that you have the major elements of equations mastered, this lesson will show you how to solve equations using isolations, distribution, and factoring.

THE MAIN THING you have to know about solving equations is this—what you do to something on one side of an equation you must do to the other side of the equation.

In order to keep the meaning of the original equation, make sure that you are doing the same thing to both sides of the equation. This means that you should perform corresponding operations on both sides of the equal sign. If you subtract 2 from the left side, you need to subtract 2 from the right side. If you divide the left side by 3, you must divide the right side by 3.

An equation is officially solved when the variable is alone (isolated) on one side of the equation and the variable is positive. Any equation with one variable can easily be solved by changing the equation this way. When you want to solve for the variable, you want to get it all by itself. This is called **isolating the variable**. To do this, you can add, subtract, multiply, or divide both sides of the equation by the same number. Let's try to isolate the variable x in the following equation:

$$25 - 2x = 35$$

Subtract 25 from both sides.

$$25 - 2x = 35$$
$$\underline{-25 \qquad -25}$$
$$-2x = 10$$

Try to divide both sides by 2.

$$\frac{-2x}{2} = \frac{10}{2}$$
$$-x = 5$$

Remember, though, the variable must be positive, so $-x = 5$ is not the answer. Remember that $-x$ is the same as $-1x$. In order to make the variable positive, divide both sides by -1.

$$x = -5$$

Let's try another one.

$$2x + 7 = 15$$

You have $2x + 7 = 15$. In order to get x by itself, first get rid of the 7. Subtract 7 from both sides.

$$2x + 7 = 15$$
$$\underline{-7 \quad -7}$$
$$2x \quad = 8$$

Now, divide both sides by 2 in order to get x by itself.

$$\frac{2x}{2} = \frac{8}{2}$$
$$x = 4$$

DISTRIBUTION AND FACTORING

The **distributive law** states that the sum of two addends multiplied by a number is the sum of the product of each addend and the number.

$$a(b + c) = ab + ac$$

....

TIP: An **addend** is any number to be added.

....

Let's look at an example. What is the value of x if $12(66) + 12(24) = x$?

Using the distributive law, x equals $12(66 + 24)$, or $12(90)$. This simplifies to 1,080.

When you use the distributive law to rewrite the expression $ab + ac$ in the form $a(b + c)$, you are **factoring** the original expression. In other words, you take the factor common to both terms of the original expression (a) and pull it out. This gives you a new "factored" version of the expression you began with.

When you use the distributive law to rewrite the expression $a(b + c)$ in the form $ab + ac$, you are **unfactoring** the original expression.

PRACTICE

Solve each algebraic equation for the variable.

1. $x + 10 = 14$

2. $a - 7 = 12$

3. $y + (-2) = 15$

4. $-r + 3 = 21$

5. $s - 9 = 3$

6. $2x = 12$

7. $-3t = -21$

8. $5q = -45$

9. $\frac{x}{4} = 3$

10. $\frac{x}{3} = 2$

11. $3a + 4 = 13$

12. $2p + 2 = 16$

13. $4(c - 1) = 12$

14. $3x - 4 = 2x + 4$

15. $10w + 14 - 8w = 12$

16. $5(b + 1) = 60$

17. $3(y - 9) - 2 = -35$

18. $4q + 12 = 16$

19. $\frac{t}{5} - 3 = -9$

20. $6(2 + f) = 5f + 15$

ANSWERS

1. Begin by asking yourself what operation is used in the equation: addition. Then, perform the inverse operation (subtraction) to both sides of the equation:

$$x + 10 = 14$$
$$\underline{-10 \quad -10}$$

Finally, combine like terms and solve for the variable.

$$x + 0 = 4$$
$$x = 4$$

2. Begin by asking yourself what operation is used in the equation: subtraction. Then, perform the inverse operation (addition) to both sides of the equation:

$$a - 7 = 12$$
$$\underline{+7 \quad +7}$$

Finally, combine like terms and solve for the variable.

$$a + 0 = 19$$
$$a = 19$$

3. Begin by asking yourself what operation is used in the equation: subtraction (addition of a negative number). Then, perform the inverse operation (addition) to both sides of the equation:

$$y + (-2) = 15$$
$$\underline{+2 \quad +2}$$

Finally, combine like terms and solve for the variable.

$$y + 0 = 17$$
$$y = 17$$

4. Begin by asking yourself what operation is used in the equation: subtraction (addition of a negative number). Then, perform the inverse operation (addition) to both sides of the equation:

$$-r + 3 = 21$$
$$\underline{-3 \quad -3}$$

Finally, combine like terms and solve for the variable.

$$-r + 0 = 18$$
$$-r = 18$$

But you want to solve for r, not $-r$. So, multiply each side by -1.

$$-r \times -1 = 18 \times -1$$
$$r = -18$$

5. Begin by asking yourself what operation is used in the equation: subtraction. Then, perform the inverse operation (addition) to both sides of the equation:

$$s - 9 = 3$$
$$\underline{+9 \quad +9}$$

Finally, combine like terms and solve for the variable.

$$s + 0 = 12$$
$$s = 12$$

6. Begin by asking yourself what operation is used in the equation: multiplication. Then, perform the inverse operation (division) to both sides of the equation:

$$2x = 12$$
$$\frac{2x}{2} = \frac{12}{2}$$

Finally, combine like terms and solve for the variable.

$$x = 6$$

7. Begin by asking yourself what operation is used in the equation: multiplication. Then, perform the inverse operation (division) to both sides of the equation:

$$-3t = -21$$
$$\frac{-3t}{-3} = \frac{-21}{-3}$$

Finally, combine like terms and solve for the variable.

$$t = 7$$

8. Begin by asking yourself what operation is used in the equation: multiplication. Then, perform the inverse operation (division) to both sides of the equation:

$$5q = -45$$
$$\frac{5q}{5} = \frac{-45}{5}$$

Finally, combine like terms and solve for the variable.

$$q = -9$$

9. Begin by asking yourself what operation is used in the equation: division. Then, perform the inverse operation (multiplication) to both sides of the equation:

$$\frac{x}{4} = 3$$
$$4 \times \frac{x}{4} = 3 \times 4$$

Finally, combine like terms and solve for the variable.

$$x = 12$$

10. Begin by asking yourself what operation is used in the equation: division. Then, perform the inverse operation (multiplication) to both sides of the equation:

$$\frac{x}{3} = 2$$
$$3 \times \frac{x}{3} = 2 \times 3$$

Finally, combine like terms and solve for the variable.

$$x = 6$$

11. Begin by performing the inverse operation for addition:

$$3a + 4 = 13$$
$$\underline{\quad -4 \quad -4 \quad}$$
$$3a + 0 = \ 9$$
$$3a = 9$$

Then, perform the inverse operation for multiplication and solve for a.

$$\frac{3a}{3} = \frac{9}{3}$$
$$a = 3$$

12. Begin by performing the inverse operation for addition:

$$2p + 2 = 16$$

$$\underline{\;-2\;\;-2}$$

$$2p\;\;\;\; = 14$$

Then, perform the inverse operation for multiplication and solve for p.

$$\frac{2p}{2} = \frac{14}{2}$$

$$p = 7$$

13. First, eliminate the parentheses by multiplying (distributing the 4):

$$4(c - 1) = 12$$

$$4c - 4 = 12$$

Then, perform the inverse operation for subtraction.

$$4c - 4 = 12$$

$$\underline{\;+4\;\;+4}$$

$$4c\;\;\;\; = 16$$

Finally, perform the inverse operation for multiplication and solve for c.

$$\frac{4c}{4} = \frac{16}{4}$$

$$c = 4$$

14. First, group the variables on one side of the equation by subtracting the smaller of the two variables from both sides:

$$3x - 4 = 2x + 4$$

$$\underline{-2x\;\;\;\;\;\;\;-2x}$$

$$x - 4 =\;\;\;\;\; 4$$

Then, perform the inverse operation for subtraction and solve for x.

$$x - 4 = 4$$

$$\underline{\;+4\;+4}$$

$$x\;\;\;\; = 8$$

15. Begin by grouping like terms together:

$$10w + 14 - 8w = 12$$

$$10w - 8w + 14 = 12$$

Combine the like terms.

$$10w - 8w = 2w$$

$$2w + 14 = 12$$

Then, perform the inverse operation for addition.

$$2w + 14 = 12$$

$$\underline{\;-14\;-14}$$

$$2w + \;0 = -2$$

$$2w = -2$$

Finally, perform the inverse operation for multiplication and solve for w.

$$\frac{2w}{2} = \frac{-2}{2}$$

$$w = -1$$

16. First, eliminate the parentheses by multiplying (distributing the 5).

$$5(b + 1) = 60$$
$$5b + 5 = 60$$

Then, perform the inverse operation for addition.

$$5b + 5 = 60$$
$$\underline{\quad -5 \quad -5 \quad}$$
$$5b + 0 = 55$$
$$5b = 55$$

Finally, perform the inverse operation for multiplication and solve for b.

$$\tfrac{5b}{5} = \tfrac{55}{5}$$
$$b = 11$$

17. First, eliminate the parentheses by multiplying (distribute the 3).

$$3(y - 9) - 2 = -35$$
$$3y - 27 - 2 = -35$$

Combine the like terms.

$$3y - 29 = -35$$

Then, perform the inverse operation for subtraction.

$$3y - 29 = -35$$
$$\underline{\quad +29 \quad +29 \quad}$$
$$3y \qquad = -6$$

Finally, perform the inverse operation for multiplication and solve for y.

$$\tfrac{3y}{3} = \tfrac{-6}{3}$$
$$y = -2$$

18. Begin by performing the inverse operation for addition.

$$4q + 12 = 16$$
$$\underline{\quad -12 \quad -12 \quad}$$
$$4q \qquad = 4$$

Then, perform the inverse operation for multiplication and solve for q.

$$\tfrac{4q}{4} = \tfrac{4}{4}$$
$$q = 1$$

19. Begin by performing the inverse operation for subtraction.

$$\tfrac{t}{5} - 3 = -9$$
$$\underline{\quad +3 \quad +3 \quad}$$
$$\tfrac{t}{5} \qquad = -6$$

Then, perform the inverse operation for division and solve for t.

$$5 \times \tfrac{t}{5} = -6 \times 5$$
$$t = -30$$

20. First, eliminate the parentheses by multiplying (distribute the 6).

$$6(2 + f) = 5f + 15$$
$$12 + 6f = 5f + 15$$

Then, group the variables on one side of the equation.

$$12 + 6f = 5f + 15$$
$$\underline{-5f \quad -5f}$$
$$12 + f = 15$$

Finally, perform the inverse operation for addition and solve for f.

$$12 + f = 15$$
$$\underline{-12 -12}$$
$$f = 3$$

inequalities

Numbers are the highest degree of knowledge.
It is knowledge itself.
—PLATO (424–348 B.C.)

In this lesson, you will learn what an inequality is and how to solve for the variable in an inequality.

HERE'S THE SCENARIO. You're saving up money for an MP3 player that costs $130. You've been pooling your allowance, part-time job pay, and monetary gifts for the past few months. You know you need at least $130. When you have saved $130 or more, you'll be able to get your MP3 player.

Question: How many numbers satisfy this requirement? In other words, how many amounts are more than $130? Your solution set would include $130 and amounts larger than $130. A question such as this can be solved using inequalities, instead of equations. It would be written as follows:

$r \geq \$130$

Inequalities are sentences that compare quantities. Inequalities contain the greater than, less than, greater than or equal to (as shown in the example), or less than or equal to symbols. The following chart visually shows the inequality symbols, as well as their verbal equivalents.

This symbol . . .	Means . . .
>	"greater than" "more than" "exceeds" "in excess of"
≥	"greater than or equal to" "no less than" "at least"
<	"less than" "fewer than" "up to"
≤	"less than or equal to" "no more than" "at most"

When you solve the inequalities for a variable, you can figure out a range of numbers that your unknown is allowed to be. Here are a few examples of inequalities:

$17 > 12$ is read "seventeen is greater than twelve."

$-61 < -35$ is read "negative sixty-one is less than negative thirty-five."

On a number line, > and < are represented by an empty circle at the end of a line segment on a number graph. When you use the symbol < or >, make an open circle at this number to show this number is not part of the solution set.

On a number line, ≥ and ≤ are represented by a solid circle at the end of a line segment on a number line graph. When you use the symbol ≤ or ≥, place a closed, or filled-in, circle at this number to show this number is a part of the solution set.

For example, the graph of the inequality $-7 \leq x < 5$ would look like this:

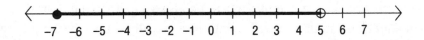

Solving an inequality means finding all of its solutions. A solution of an inequality is a number that can be substituted for a variable and makes the inequality true.

You can change an inequality in the same way you can change an equation—you can add the same number to both sides, subtract the same number, and so on. There is, however, one rule that you need to remember when you deal with inequalities:

When you multiply or divide by a negative number, you need to reverse the inequality sign.

If $x > y$, then $-x < -y$. Let's see how this works: $-5x + 3 > 28$ can also be expressed as which of the following? Remember, the goal is to isolate the variable x.

$$-5x + 3 > 28$$
$$\underline{\quad\quad -3 \; -3\quad}$$
$$-5x \quad\;\; > 25$$

Okay, time to apply the rule. When you multiply or divide by a negative number, you need to reverse the sign. So when you divide by -5, you get:

$$\tfrac{-5x}{-5} > \tfrac{25}{-5}$$
$$x < -5$$

To graph a solution set on a number line, use the number in the solution as the starting point on the number line. In the problem $x < -5$, the starting point on the number line is -5. Because the symbol $<$ is used, make an open circle at this number to show this number is not part of the solution set. Next, draw an arrow from that point to the left on the number line, because solutions to this problem are less than -5.

Let's try another one. Solve for x:

$$12 - 6x > 0$$

First, you need to subtract 12 from both sides.

$$12 - 6x > 0$$
$$\underline{-12 \quad\;\; -12\quad}$$
$$-6x > -12$$

Now, divide both sides by –6. Notice that the sign flips this time, because you are dividing by a negative number.

$$\frac{-6x}{-6} < \frac{-12}{-6}$$

$$x < 2$$

To graph this solution set on a number line, 2 is the starting point. Because the symbol < is used, make an open circle and draw an arrow from that point to the left on the number line.

You could solve for x in this inequality without ever multiplying or dividing by a negative number. How? Just add $6x$ to both sides and the sign stays the same. Then, divide both sides by 6.

$$12 - 6x > 0$$
$$\underline{+6x\ +6x}$$
$$12\qquad > 6x$$
$$\frac{12}{6} > \frac{6x}{6}$$
$$2 > x$$

SOLVING COMPOUND INEQUALITIES

A **compound inequality** is a combination of two or more inequalities, such as $-3 < x + 1 < 4$. How would you solve this?

Start by subtracting 1 from all parts of the inequality to get the variable by itself:

$$-3 - 1 < x + 1 - 1 < 4 - 1$$
$$-4 < x < 3$$

The solution set for this compound inequality is all numbers between –4 and 3. On a number line, the solution set looks like this:

PRACTICE

1. Draw the solution set of $x \le 4$ on the following number line.

2. What inequality is represented by the graph?

3. What is the solution of the inequality $3x > 9$?

4. Which of the following is the solution of the inequality $-6a - 4 \ge 8$?

5. What compound inequality is shown in the graph?

6. Draw a number line for the compound inequality $x > 6$ or $x \le -3$.

ANSWERS

1.

Create a number line for the solution to the inequality *x is less than or equal to 4*. This is a graph with a closed circle at 4 and the arrow pointing to the left.

2. In this number line, there is an open circle at -3, so the symbol in the inequality is either $<$ or $>$. The arrow is pointing to the right toward numbers greater than -3. Therefore, the inequality representing the graph is *y is greater than -3*, which is written as $y > -3$.

3. Solve for x as you would in an equation. Divide each side of the inequality by 3: $\frac{3x}{3} > \frac{9}{3}$. The solution is $x > 3$.

4. Solve for a as you would in an equation. Add 4 to both sides of the inequality.

$$-6a - 4 + 4 \geq 8 + 4$$
$$-6a \geq 12$$
$$\frac{-6a}{-6} \geq \frac{12}{-6}$$

Remember to switch the direction of the inequality symbol because you are dividing both sides by a negative number. The answer is $a \leq -2$.

5. This graph shows that the solution set is all numbers between –4 and 9, and includes –4 because of the closed circle. In the solution set are numbers that are *greater than or equal to –4* and, at the same time, *less than 9*.

6.

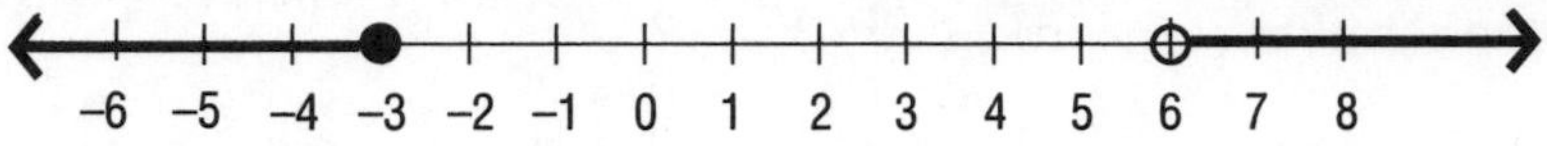

```
<----+--+--+--●--+--+--+--+--+--+--+--⊕--+--+---->
    -6 -5 -4 -3 -2 -1  0  1  2  3  4  5  6  7  8
```

You need to create a number line for a compound inequality that shows two inequalities at once on the same graph. The inequality $x > 6$ has an open circle at 6 and an arrow to the right. The other inequality, $x \leq -3$, has a closed circle at –3 and an arrow pointing to the left.

powers and exponents

This lesson will uncover important properties of powers and exponents. You will discover how to simplify and evaluate various types of exponents.

HOW DO YOU raise numbers to different **powers**? Well, let's look at an example. In 3^2, we call 3 the **base** and 2 the **exponent**.

$3^2 = 3 \times 3 = 9$

When you raise integers to different powers, it is important to remember the following rules:

- Raising a number greater than 1 to a power greater than 1 results in a bigger number: $2^2 = 4$
- Raising a fraction between 0 and 1 to a power greater than 1 results in a smaller number: $(\frac{1}{2})^2 = \frac{1}{4}$
- A positive or negative integer raised to the power of 0 is always equal to 1: $9^0 = 1$
- A positive integer raised to any power is equal to a positive number: $9^2 = 9 \times 9 = 81$
- A negative integer raised to any even power is equal to a positive number: $(-8)^2 = -8 \times -8 = 64$

- A negative integer raised to any odd power is equal to a negative number: $(-3)^3 = -3 \times -3 \times -3 = 9 \times -3 = -27$
- A positive or negative integer raised to a negative power is always less than 1: $4^{-5} = \frac{1}{4^5}$

Think of exponents as a shorthand way of writing math. Instead of writing $2 \times 2 \times 2 \times 2$, you can write 2^4. This saves time and energy—plus, it means the same thing!

....

TIP: Exponents are often used in algebraic expressions. In s^5, s is the base and 5 is the exponent. In expanded form, this means $s \cdot s \cdot s \cdot s \cdot s$. The expression pr^2 represents $p \cdot r \cdot r$ in expanded form. The variable p is a base with an exponent of 1 and r is a base with an exponent of 2.

....

OPERATIONS AND EXPONENTS

When you multiply powers of the same base, add the exponents:

$$2^2 \times 2^3 = 2^{2+3} = 2^5$$

Think of it this way: $2^2 \times 2^3 = (2 \times 2) \times (2 \times 2 \times 2)$, which is the same as 2^5.

When you divide powers of the same base, subtract the exponents:

$$3^8 \div 3^2 = 3^{8-2} = 3^6$$

When you raise a power to a power, multiply the exponents:

$$(5^3)^4 = 5^{3 \cdot 4} = 5^{12}$$

Bottom line: If you're in doubt when multiplying or dividing powers, expand it out! Not sure about $2^2 \times 2^4$? Rewrite it as $(2 \times 2)(2 \times 2 \times 2 \times 2)$, which is $2 \times 2 \times 2 \times 2 \times 2 \times 2$, or 2^6.

When there are multiple bases inside parentheses that are being raised to a power, each base in the parentheses must be evaluated with that power. Try to simplify the following:

$(2x^2y^3)^3$

$2^3x^{2 \cdot 3}y^{3 \cdot 3}$

$8x^6y^9$

The exponent outside the parentheses was evaluated on each base—2, x, and y.

DIFFERENT BASES

When you do not have the same base, try to convert to the same base:

$25^4 \times 5^{12} = (5^2)^4 \times 5^{12} = 5^8 \times 5^{12} = 5^{20}$

Try solving for x in the following equation:

$2^{x+2} = 8^3$

First, get the base numbers equal. Because 8 can be expressed as 2^3, then $8^3 = (2^3)^3 = 2^9$. Both sides of the equation have a common base of 2, $2^{x+2} = 2^9$, so set the exponents equal to each other to solve for x: $x + 2 = 9$. So, $x = 7$.

NEGATIVE EXPONENTS

Any base number raised to a negative exponent is the reciprocal of the base raised to a positive exponent. Confused? Let's look at a real example:

$3^{-2} = (\frac{1}{3})^2 = \frac{1}{9}$

When simplifying with negative exponents, remember that $a^{-b} = \frac{1}{a^b}$.

PRACTICE

1. Evaluate 6^4.

2. Circle the expression that is NOT equivalent to $5 \cdot 5 \cdot 5 \cdot 5$.

$5 \cdot 4$

$(5 \cdot 5)^2$

5^4

$5 \cdot 5^3$

625

3. Evaluate $cd^2 - 1$ when $c = -1$ and $d = -6$.

4. The expression 4^{-2} is equivalent to ____.

5. How can you simplify the expression $2^2 \cdot 2^3$?

6. Simplify: $a^2b \cdot ab^3$

7. Simplify: $\dfrac{x^6}{x^3}$

8. Simplify: $(3xy^3)^2$

ANSWERS

1. 6^4 is equal to $6 \cdot 6 \cdot 6 \cdot 6$. When multiplied together, the result is 1,296.

2. $5 \cdot 4$ should be circled. This is equal to 20. The others are equivalent to 625.

3. Substitute the values for the variables in the expression:

$(-1)(-6)^2 - 1$

Evaluate the exponent:

$(-1)(-6)^2 - 1$

Remember that $(-6)^2 = (-6)(-6) = 36$.

Multiply the first term: $(-1)(36) - 1$

This simplifies to $(-36) - 1$. Evaluate by changing subtraction to addition and the sign of the second term to its opposite. Signs are the same, so add and keep the sign:

$(-36) + (-1) = -37$

4. When you evaluate a negative exponent, take the reciprocal of the base and make the exponent positive. Therefore, 4^{-2} is equivalent to $\frac{1}{4^2}$, which simplifies to $\frac{1}{16}$.

5. When you multiply like bases, add the exponents. The expression $2^2 \cdot 2^3$ is equivalent to 2^{2+3}, which simplifies to 2^5.

6. When you multiply like bases, add the exponents. The expression $a^2b \cdot ab^3$ can also be written as $a^2b^1 \cdot a^1b^3$. Grouping like bases results in $a^2a^1 \cdot b^1b^3$. Adding the exponents gives $a^{2+1}b^{1+3}$, which is equal to a^3b^4, the simplified answer.

7. When you divide like bases, subtract the exponents. The expression $\frac{x^6}{x^3}$ then becomes x^{6-3}, which simplifies to x^3.

8. When you raise a quantity to a power, raise each base to that power by multiplying the exponents. The expression $(3xy^3)^2$ equals $3^2x^2y^6$, which simplifies to $9x^2y^6$. Another way to look at this problem is to remember that when a quantity is squared, it is multiplied by itself. The expression $(3xy^3)^2$ becomes $(3xy^3) \cdot (3xy^3)$. Multiply coefficients and add the exponents of like bases: $3 \cdot 3x^{1+1}y^{3+3}$ simplifies to $9x^2y^6$.

scientific notation

> *I believe there are 15,747,724,136,275,002,577,605,653,*
> *961,181,555,468,044,717,914,527,116,709,366,231,425,076,*
> *185,631,031,296 protons in the universe and*
> *the same number of electrons.*
> —SIR ARTHUR EDDINGTON (1882–1944)

How could you write the number 57,000,000,000 in a shorter, quicker way? This lesson will teach you about scientific notation and its advantages. Scientific notation is used to lessen the chance of leaving out a zero or misplacing a decimal point.

IN THE PAST, scientists found themselves with a problem when they had to work with really big numbers like 57,000,000,000 or really little numbers like 0.000000057. You see, scientists measure very large numbers, such as the distance from Earth to the sun, or very small numbers, such as the diameter of an electron.

To combat dealing with so many zeros, they came up with the idea to use shorthand to represent such extreme numbers. The shorthand, known as **scientific notation**, uses the powers of ten.

10^0	= 1
10^1	= 10
10^2	= 100
10^3	= 1,000
10^4	= 10,000
10^5	= 100,000
10^6	= 1,000,000 *one million*
10^7	= 10,000,000
10^8	= 100,000,000
10^9	= 1,000,000,000 *one billion*
10^{10}	= 10,000,000,000
10^{11}	= 100,000,000,000
10^{12}	= 1,000,000,000,000 *one trillion*
10^{13}	= 10,000,000,000,000
10^{14}	= 100,000,000,000,000

With scientific notation, instead of writing 57,000,000,000, you could write 5.7×10^{10}. Instead of writing 0.000000057, you could write 5.7×10^{-8}. The exponent of 10 tells whether the number is really big (a positive exponent) or really small (negative exponent).

The absolute value of the exponent tells how far the decimal point was moved to fit the pattern. Look at 7^{-9}. The absolute value of –9 is 9, so you know the decimal point moved nine places:

$$.000000007$$

To master scientific notation, you do not have to memorize the notation table. The trick to expressing a large number as a power of 10 is to move the decimal place over as many spaces as it takes for there to be one unit to the left of it. Then, add "× 10" and raise the 10 to the power that represents the number of times you moved the decimal point. Look at a huge number like

830,000,000,000,000 and count the places you'll need to move the decimal point.

830,000,000,000,000.

You counted over 14 places, so $830,000,000,000,000 = 8.3 \times 10^{14}$.

Let's try another example. Express 795,000,000 in scientific notation.

795,000,000.

You counted over eight places, so $795,000,000 = 7.95 \times 10^8$.

Let's try this in reverse. Express 3.483×10^5 in standard form. You need to move the decimal point over the same as the power indicates. In this case, it would move five places.

3.483 . . . ?

Wondering how to do this when there are only three numbers shown to the right of the decimal place? Don't forget, you can use zeros as placeholders next to that 3. Actually, there are an unlimited number of zeros after that 3. But, you need to move only two more spaces:

3.48300

3.483×10^5 in standard form is 348,300.

PRACTICE

1. What is 7.206×10^{-4} written in standard form?

2. What is 567,090,000 written in scientific notation?

3. Write 2.701×10^7 in standard form.

4. Write 4.09×10^{-5} in standard form.

5. Write 5,063,000,000 in scientific notation.

ANSWERS

1. .0007206. The negative exponent of 4 dictates that you move the decimal point four places to the left.
2. 5.6709×10^8. Change the large number to be a decimal number between 1 and 10, followed by a multiplication by a power of 10. By doing this, you have moved the decimal point eight places to the left.
3. The exponent of 7 on the power of 10 dictates that you move the decimal point in the decimal 2.701 seven places to the right. Three of the places will be taken up by the digits 7, 0, and 1 and then four more zeros will follow to result in 27,010,000.
4. The negative exponent, –5, on the power of 10 means that you must move the decimal point five places to the left. The number 4.09 has only one digit to the left of the decimal point. Four leading zeros must be added as placeholders: 0.0000409.
5. Write the number as a decimal between one and ten, and then multiply by the appropriate power of 10. Move the decimal point nine places to the left to go from 5,063,000,000 to 5.063. The answer is 5.063×10^9.

square roots

Math is radical!
—BUMPER STICKER

This lesson exposes the meaning behind the sneaky √ symbol. What are roots and radicals? How can you estimate them?

TAKING THE square root (also called a **radical**) is the way to undo the exponent from an equation like $2^2 = 4$. If $2^2 = 4$, then 2 is the square root of 4 and $\sqrt{4}$ = 2. The exponent in 2^2 tells you to square 2. You multiply $2 \cdot 2$ and get $2^2 = 4$.

The **radical sign** √ indicates that you are to find the square root of the number beneath it. The number inside the radical sign is called the **radicand**. For example, in $\sqrt{9}$, the radicand is 9.

A positive square root of a number is called the **principal square root**. For $\sqrt{9}$, $3 \times 3 = 9$, so 3 is the principal square root.

A negative sign outside the radical sign means the **negative square root**. For example, $\sqrt{9} = 3$, but $-\sqrt{9} = -3$.

PERFECT SQUARES

The easiest radicands to deal with are perfect squares. A **perfect square** is a number with an integer for a square root. For example, 25 is a perfect square because its square root is 5, but 24 is not a perfect square because it doesn't have an integer for a square root. (No number multiplied by itself equals 24.)

Because they appear so often, it is useful to learn to recognize the first few perfect squares:

$$0^2 = 0$$
$$1^2 = 1$$
$$2^2 = 4$$
$$3^2 = 9$$
$$4^2 = 16$$
$$5^2 = 25$$
$$6^2 = 36$$
$$7^2 = 49$$
$$8^2 = 64$$
$$9^2 = 81$$
$$10^2 = 100$$
$$11^2 = 121$$
$$12^2 = 144$$

It is even easier to recognize when a variable is a perfect square because the exponent is even. For example, $x^{14} = x^7 \cdot x^7$ and $a^8 = a^4 \cdot a^4$.

....

TIP: You can use known perfect squares to estimate other square roots. Suppose you were asked to determine $\sqrt{50}$. What is the closest perfect square to 50? Try a few numbers to see:

$6 \times 6 = 36$
Too low.
$8 \times 8 = 64$
Too high.
$7 \times 7 = 49$
Perfect.

So, you can determine that $\sqrt{50}$ is going to be between 7 and 8, much closer to 7.

....

To determine if a radicand contains any factors that are perfect squares, factor the radicand completely. All the factors must be prime. A number is prime if its only factors are 1 and the number itself. A prime number cannot be factored any further. Let's try determining the square root of the following:

$$\sqrt{64x^2y^{10}}$$

Write the number under the radical sign as a square:

$$\sqrt{8xy^5 \cdot 8xy^5}$$

Because you have two identical terms multiplied by each other, you know this is a perfect square. Evaluate to find the final solution: $8xy^5$. You could also have split the radical into parts and evaluated them separately.

Let's try another one. Find the square root of $\sqrt{64x^2y^{10}}$.

First, split the terms:

$$\sqrt{64 \cdot x^2 \cdot y^{10}}$$

Each term is a perfect square. Write as squares:

$$\sqrt{8 \cdot 8} \cdot \sqrt{x \cdot x} \cdot \sqrt{y^5 \cdot y^5}$$

Finally, evaluate each new radical:

$$8 \cdot x \cdot y^5$$
$$8xy^5$$

PRACTICE 1

Solve the following problems.

1. $\sqrt{49} =$

2. $\sqrt{81} =$

3. $\sqrt{144} =$

4. $-\sqrt{64} =$

5. $4\sqrt{4} =$

6. $-2\sqrt{9} =$

7. $\sqrt{a^2} =$

8. $5\sqrt{36} =$

SIMPLIFYING RADICALS

Not all radicands are perfect squares. There is no whole number that, when multiplied by itself, equals 5. With a calculator, you can get a decimal that squares very close to 5, but it won't come out exactly. The only precise way to represent the square root of five is to write $\sqrt{5}$. It cannot be simplified any further.

There are three rules for knowing when a radical cannot be simplified any further:

1. The radicand contains no factor, other than 1, that is a perfect square.
2. The radicand cannot be a fraction.
3. The radical cannot be in the denominator of a fraction.

ADDING AND SUBTRACTING

Square roots are easy to add or subtract. You can add or subtract radicals if the radicands are the same. To add or subtract radicals, add the number in front of the radicals and leave the radicand the same. When you add $15\sqrt{2}$ and $5\sqrt{2}$, you add the 15 and the 5, but the radicand $\sqrt{2}$ stays the same. The answer is $20\sqrt{2}$.

PRACTICE 2

Solve the following problems.

1. $3\sqrt{7} + 8\sqrt{7} =$

2. $11\sqrt{3} - 8\sqrt{3} =$

3. $5\sqrt{2} + 6\sqrt{2} - 3\sqrt{2} =$

MULTIPLYING AND DIVIDING RADICALS

To multiply radicals like $4\sqrt{3}$ and $2\sqrt{2}$, multiply the numbers in front of the radicals: 4 times 2. Then, multiply the radicands: 3 times 2. The answer is $8\sqrt{6}$.

Try the following:

$$5\sqrt{3} \cdot 2\sqrt{2}$$

Multiply the numbers in front of the radicals. Then, multiply the radicands. You will end up with $10\sqrt{6}$.

To divide the radical $4\sqrt{6}$ by $2\sqrt{3}$, divide the numbers in front of the radicals. Then, divide the radicands. The answer is $2\sqrt{2}$.

As opposed to adding or subtracting, the radicands do not have to be the same when you multiply or divide radicals.

PRACTICE 3

Solve the following problems.

1. $7\sqrt{3} \cdot 5\sqrt{2}$

2. $\dfrac{14\sqrt{6}}{7\sqrt{2}}$

3. $-3\sqrt{5} \cdot 4\sqrt{2}$

ANSWERS

Practice 1

1. 7
2. 9
3. 12
4. –8
5. 8
6. –6
7. a
8. 30

Practice 2

1. $3\sqrt{7} + 8\sqrt{7} = 11\sqrt{7}$
2. $11\sqrt{3} - 8\sqrt{3} = 3\sqrt{3}$
3. $5\sqrt{2} + 6\sqrt{2} - 3\sqrt{2} = 8\sqrt{2}$

Practice 3

1. $7\sqrt{3} \cdot 5\sqrt{2} = 35\sqrt{6}$
2. $\dfrac{14\sqrt{6}}{7\sqrt{2}} = 2\sqrt{3}$
3. $-3\sqrt{5} \cdot 4\sqrt{2} = -12\sqrt{10}$

algebraic expressions and word problems

"What's one and one and one and one and one and one and one and one and one and one?"
"I don't know," said Alice. "I lost count."
—LEWIS CARROLL (1832–1898)

In this lesson, you'll see that translating word problems into algebra is important for both math tests and issues that arise every day. Specifically, you'll learn to tackle distance, mixture, and work problems.

WHEN YOU ARE translating sentences and word problems into algebraic expressions and equations, it can seem like you are translating between two different languages.

There are some strategies, however, that will help you become fluent in both:

- First, read the problem to determine what you are looking for.
- Then, write the amount you are looking for in terms of x (or whatever letter you want to use). You can do this by writing "Let $x = \ldots$" Write any other unknown amounts in terms of x, too.
- Last, set up the algebraic expressions in an equation with an equals sign and solve for the variable.

TIP: When you are translating key words in an algebraic expression, the phrases *less than* and *greater than* do not translate in the same order as they are written in the sentence. For example, when you are translating the expression *eight less than 15*, the correct expression is 15 − 8, not 8 − 15.

Study the following to see how to translate word problems into mathematical statements and equations.

EQUALS KEY WORDS:
IS, ARE, HAS, WAS, WERE, HAD

English	Math
Casey is 13 years old.	$C = 13$
There are 15 skate shoes.	$S = 15$
Jenny has 5 acoustic guitars.	$J = 5$

ADDITION KEY WORDS: *SUM; TOGETHER; TOTAL;*
MORE, GREATER, OR *OLDER THAN*

English	Math
The sum of two numbers is 10.	$x + y = 10$
Karen has $5 more than Sam.	$K = 5 + S$
Judi is 2 years older than Tony.	$J = T + 2$
The total of the three numbers is 25.	$a + b + c = 25$
Joan and Tom together have $16.	$J + T = 16$

SUBTRACTION KEY WORDS: *DIFFERENCE; LESS, FEWER,*
OR *YOUNGER THAN; REMAIN; LEFT OVER*

English	Math
The difference between the two numbers is 17.	$x - y = 17$
Mike has 5 fewer cats than twice the number Jan has.	$M = 2J - 5$
Jay is 2 years younger than Brett.	$J = B - 2$
After Carol ate 3 apples, R apples remained.	$R = C - 3$

MULTIPLICATION KEY WORDS: *PRODUCT, TIMES, OF*

English	Math
20% of the students	$\frac{20}{100} \times S$
Half of the boys	$\frac{1}{2} \times b$
The product of two numbers is 12.	$a \times b = 12$ or $ab = 12$

DIVISION KEY WORDS: *PER, EVENLY*

English	Math
15 drops per teaspoon	15 drops/tsp.
22 miles per gallon	22 miles/gal.
100 gifts divided evenly among 10 people	$100 \div 10$

Look at an example where knowing the key words is necessary:

Twenty less than five times a number is equal to the product of ten and the number. What is the number?

Let's let x equal the number we are trying to find. Now, translate the sentence piece by piece, and then solve the equation.

Twenty less than five times a number equals the product of 10 and x.

$$5x - 20 \qquad\qquad = \qquad\qquad 10x$$

The equation is $5x - 20 = 10x$. Subtract $5x$ from both sides:

$$5x - 5x - 20 = 10x - 5x$$

Now, divide both sides by 5:

$$\frac{-20}{5} = \frac{5x}{5}$$
$$-4 = x$$

In this example, the key words *less than* tell you to subtract from the number and the key word *product* reminds you to multiply.

PROBLEM SOLVING WITH WORD PROBLEMS

There are a variety of different types of word problems you will encounter on tests or in your daily life. To help with these types of problems, always begin first by figuring out what you need to solve for and defining your variable(s) as what is unknown. Then write and solve an equation that matches the question asked.

Distance word problems use the distance formula rate × time = distance. Distance formula problems include key words such as *speed*, *plane*, *train*, *boat*, *car*, *walk*, *run*, *climb*, and *swim*. They provide two of the three elements—rate, time, and distance—in the distance formula. Plug those two elements into the formula and solve for the third. Don't forget that rate and time have to be measured in common units. If the rate is measured in miles per hour, the time has to be measured in hours, not minutes or days.

Let's practice:

How far did the plane travel in 4 hours if it traveled at an average speed of 300 miles per hour?

$rt = d$

$r = 300$

$t = 4$

$300 \times 4 = d$

$1,200 = d$

The plane traveled 1,200 miles.

Mixture questions will present you with two or more different types of "objects" to be mixed together. Some common types of mixture scenarios are combining different amounts of money at different interest rates, different amounts of solutions at different concentrations, and different amounts of food (candy, soda, etc.) that have different prices per pound. Let's put this into play:

How many pounds of hot chocolate that costs $4 per pound need to be mixed with 10 pounds of hot chocolate that costs $6.40 per pound to create a mixture of hot chocolate that costs $5.50 per pound?

For this type of question, remember that the total amount spent in each case will be the price per pound times how many pounds in the mixture. Therefore, if you let x = the number of pounds of $4 hot chocolate, then $4(x)$ is the amount of money spent on $4 hot chocolate, $6.40(10) is the amount spent on $6.40 hot chocolate, and $5.50(x + 10)$ is the total amount spent. Write an equation that adds the first two amounts and sets it equal to the total amount. Then, multiply through the equation:

$$4(x) + 6.40(10) = 5.50(x + 10)$$
$$4x + 64 = 5.5x + 55$$

Subtract $4x$ from both sides:

$$4x - 4x + 64 = 5.5x - 4x + 55$$

Subtract 55 from both sides:

$$64 - 55 = 1.5x + 55 - 55$$

Divide both sides by 1.5:

$$\frac{9}{1.5} = \frac{1.5x}{1.5}$$
$$6 = x$$

You need 6 pounds of the $4 per pound hot chocolate.

Work problems often present the scenario of two people working to complete the same job. To solve this particular type of problem, think about how much of the job will be completed in one hour. For example, if someone can complete a job in 5 hours, then $\frac{1}{5}$ of the job is completed in 1 hour. If a person can complete a job in x hours, then $\frac{1}{x}$ of the job is completed in 1 hour. Take a look at the next example to see how this is used to solve work problems:

Jason can mow a lawn in 2 hours. Shantelle can mow the same lawn in 4 hours. If they work together, how many hours will it take them to mow the same lawn?

Think about how much of the lawn each person completes individually. Jason can finish in 2 hours, so in 1 hour he completes $\frac{1}{2}$ of the lawn. Because Shantelle can finish in 4 hours, then in 1 hour she completes $\frac{1}{4}$ of the lawn. If we let $x =$ the time it takes both Jason and Shantelle working together, then $\frac{1}{x}$ is the amount of the lawn they finish in 1 hour working together. Then use the equation $\frac{1}{2} + \frac{1}{4} = \frac{1}{x}$ and solve for x. Multiply each term by the least common denominator (LCD) of $4x$:

$$4x(\tfrac{1}{2}) + 4x(\tfrac{1}{4}) = 4x(\tfrac{1}{x})$$

The equation becomes $2x + x = 4$. Combine like terms and divide each side by 3.

$$3x = 4$$
$$\frac{3x}{3} = \frac{4}{3}$$

So, $x = 1\frac{1}{3}$ hours. Because $\frac{1}{3}$ of an hour is $\frac{1}{3}$ of 60 minutes, which is 20 minutes, the correct answer is 1 hour and 20 minutes.

PRACTICE

1. Ben walked 20 miles in 4 hours. What was his average speed?

2. Jim and Bryan can shovel the driveway together in 6 hours. If it takes Jim 10 hours working alone, how long will it take Bryan working alone?

3. The sixth-grade class bought two different types of candy to sell at a school fund-raiser. They purchased 50 pounds of candy at $2.25 per pound and x pounds at $1.90 per pound. What is the total number of pounds they bought if the total amount of money spent on candy was $169.50?

ANSWERS

1. Use the distance formula and substitute in the known values:
$$rt = d$$
$$t = 4$$
$$d = 20$$
$$r \times 4 = 20$$
Now, isolate the variable to find the speed:
$$(r \times 4) \div 4 = 20 \div 4$$
$$r = 5$$
Ben walked at a rate of 5 miles per hour.

2. Let x = the number of hours Bryan takes to shovel the driveway by himself. In 1 hour, Bryan can do $\frac{1}{x}$ of the work and Jim can do $\frac{1}{10}$ of the work. As an equation this looks like $\frac{1}{x} + \frac{1}{10} = \frac{1}{6}$, where $\frac{1}{6}$ represents what part they can shovel in 1 hour together. Multiply both sides of the equation by the least common denominator, $30x$, to get an equation of $30 + 3x = 5x$. Subtract $3x$ from both sides of the equation: $30 + 3x - 3x = 5x - 3x$. This simplifies to $30 = 2x$. Divide both sides of the equal sign by 2 to get a solution of 15 hours.

3. Let x = the amount of candy at \$1.90 per pound. Let y = the total number of pounds of candy purchased. If there are also 50 pounds of candy at \$2.25 per pound, then the total amount of candy can be expressed as $y = x + 50$. Use the equation $1.90x + 2.25(50) = \$169.50$ because the total amount of money spent was \$169.50. Multiply on the left side: $1.90x + 112.50 = 169.50$. Subtract 112.50 from both sides: $1.90x + 112.50 - 112.50 = 169.50 - 112.50$. Divide both sides by 1.90: $\frac{1.90x}{1.90} = \frac{57}{1.90}$. So, $x = 30$ pounds, which is the amount of candy that costs \$1.90 per pound. The total amount of candy is $30 + 50$, which is 80 pounds.

SECTION 3

basic geometry—
all shapes and sizes

GEOMETRY IS THE member of the math family that deals with one- and two-dimensional figures. You encounter these figures every day—from the tires on your bike to perpendicular streets in your neighborhood.

In geometry, there are important formulas that are used to measure the shape, size, or other properties of these one- and two-dimensional figures. Although these formulas are used by the "professionals" in fields such as architecture and carpentry, you can apply them to everyday geometry puzzles. You are using geometry formulas when you determine how many cans of paint you need to cover your bedroom walls or what angle you need to hang a bookshelf. In school, geometry will help you figure out how much paper you need to make a book jacket for your math textbook. When you look up at the night sky, geometry even helps you locate the stars.

This section will introduce you to the basic concepts of geometry, including:

- lines
- angles
- quadrilaterals
- perimeter
- area
- symmetry
- similarity
- triangles
- circles
- circumference

138   basic geometry

- three-dimensional figures
- volume
- surface area
- the coordinate plane
- slope of a line

lines and angles

There is geometry in the humming of the strings.
—PYTHAGORAS (580–500 B.C.)

Let's learn the lingo of lines and angles.

ANGLES CAN BE measured with a tool called the **protractor**.

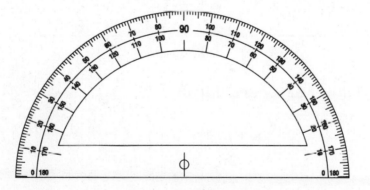

A **line** is 180 degrees and can be thought of as a perfectly flat angle.

A **ray** is part of a line that has one endpoint. It extends indefinitely in one direction.

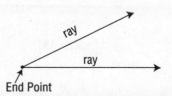

ray

ray

End Point

An **acute angle** is less than 90°.

Acute Angle

A **right angle** equals 90°.

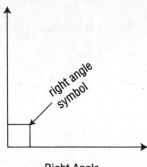

Right Angle

A **straight line** is 180°.

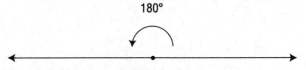

Straight Angle

An **obtuse angle** is greater that 90°.

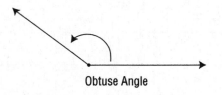

Obtuse Angle

Two angles are **supplementary** if they add to 180°.

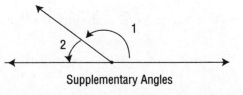

Supplementary Angles

$\angle 1 + \angle 2 = 180°$

Two angles are **complementary** if they add to 90°.

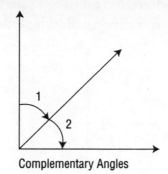

Complementary Angles

If you **bisect** an angle, you cut it exactly in half. This forms **congruent** angles, which have the same measure.

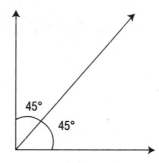

When two lines intersect, four angles are formed. The sum of these angles is 360 degrees.

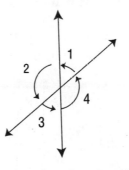

∠1 + ∠2 + ∠3 + ∠4 = 360°

When two lines are perpendicular to each other, their intersection forms four 90-degree angles, which are also called **right angles**. Right angles are identified by little boxes at the intersection of the angle's arms.

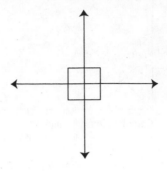

Perpendicular Lines

When lines are **parallel**, they never meet.

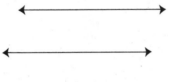

Parallel Lines

A **transversal** is a line that intersects two or more other lines. In the following figure, angles 1, 3, 5, and 7 are equal. Angles 2, 4, 6, and 8 are equal. Angles 1 and 7 and 2 and 8 are called **alternate exterior angles**. Angles 3 and 5 and 4 and 6 are called **alternate interior angles**.

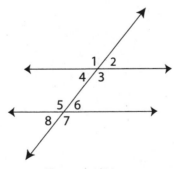

Transversal Lines

Vertical angles are the angles across from each other that are formed by intersecting lines. Vertical lines are always equal. In the following figure, angles 1 and 3 are equal vertical angles and angles 2 and 4 are equal vertical angles.

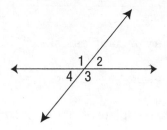

PRACTICE

Use the following images to complete questions 1 and 2.

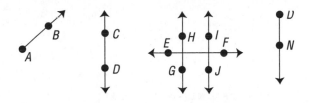

1. Circle the ray(s).

2. Draw a square around the line(s).

Use the following images to complete questions 3–6.

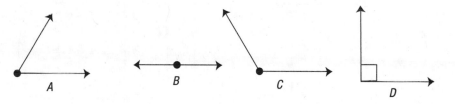

3. Which angle is acute?

4. Which angle is a right angle?

5. Which angle is a straight line?

6. Which angle is obtuse?

Use the following image to complete questions 7 and 8.

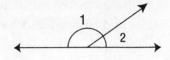

7. Is angle 1 supplementary or complementary?

8. Are they congruent angles?

Use the following image to complete question 9.

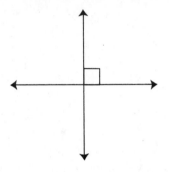

9. Are the above lines perpendicular or parallel?

ANSWERS

1. See circles below.
2. See squares below.

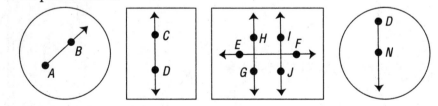

3. *A*
4. *D*
5. *B*
6. *C*
7. supplementary
8. No, they are not equal angles.
9. perpendicular

quadrilaterals

Do not worry about your difficulties in mathematics,
I assure you that mine are greater.
—ALBERT EINSTEIN (1879–1955)

In this lesson, you will learn about a shape called a quadrilateral, which is famous for having four sides. *Quadri* or *quattor* means "four" in Latin, and *lateral* means "side," so when we say a shape is a quadrilateral, we mean it has four sides. A quadrilateral can be further classified into many different forms, but here we will focus on the most important family of quadrilaterals—trapezoids and parallelograms, along with their sub-shapes.

A QUADRILATERAL IS a two-dimensional closed shape with four sides. A line drawn from one vertex of a quadrilateral to the opposite vertex is called a **diagonal**.

TYPES OF QUADRILATERALS

A quadrilateral with one pair of parallel sides (bases) is called a **trapezoid**. In an isosceles trapezoid, the sides that are not bases are congruent. Because the parallel bases are not the same length in a trapezoid, we call these bases b_1 and b_2. Trapezoids have exactly *one* pair of parallel sides.

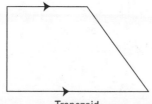

Trapezoid

Parallelograms have *two* pairs of parallel sides. The opposite sides are congruent. The opposite angles are congruent. The diagonals of parallelograms bisect each other.

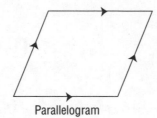
Parallelogram

Parallelograms are broken down into further subgroups.

Rectangles are parallelograms with four right angles. This means that the diagonals of a rectangle bisect each other.

Rectangle

A **rhombus** is a parallelogram with four congruent sides. The diagonals of a rhombus bisect not only each other, but also the angles that they connect! Also, the diagonals are perpendicular.

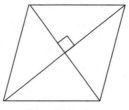
Rhombus

A **square** is a rhombus with four right angles.

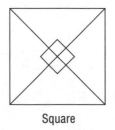
Square

PRACTICE

1. Identify all the names that describe this quadrilateral.

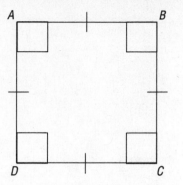

2. Find the value of x in this parallelogram.

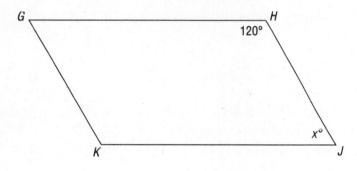

ANSWERS

1. Parallelogram; opposite sides are equal.
   Rectangle; it has four right angles.
   Rhombus; all sides are congruent.
   Square; the sides are congruent and the angles are all 90 degrees.
2. The opposite angles are equal. Because angle H is 120 degrees, angle K must also be 120 degrees. There are 360 degrees in any quadrilateral, so the other angles (G and J) must add up to $360 - 120$ (angle K) $- 120$ (angle H):
   $$360 - 120 - 120 = 120$$
   Angles G and J are equal, so to find x, divide 120 by 2: $x = 60$ degrees.

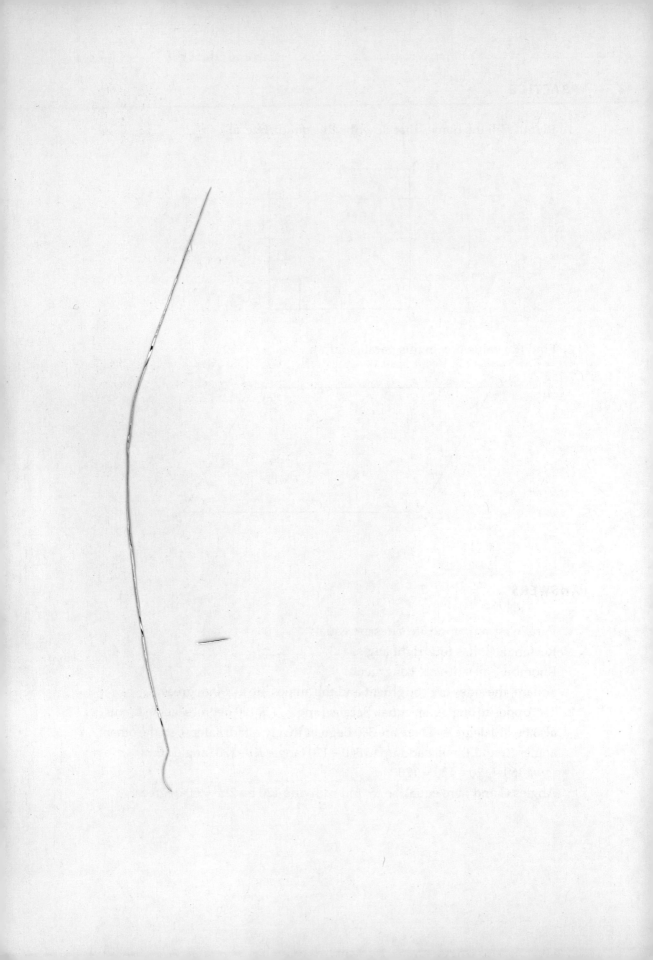

perimeter

With me everything turns into mathematics.
—RENÉ DESCARTES (1596–1650)

This lesson will describe ways that geometry is used for measuring, specifically perimeter. Perimeter has many uses in real life outside of your math classroom.

WHEN YOU MEASURE the distance around a noncircular shape, you are finding its **perimeter**.

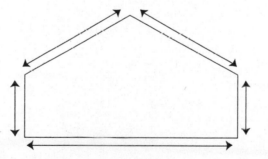

Perimeter is an addition concept; it is a linear, one-dimensional measurement.

To find the perimeter of a noncircular shape, add up all of the lengths of the sides of the figure. Be sure to name the units.

The perimeter of a **square**, or any rhombus, is equal to 4s, where s is the length of a side. Because all four sides are equal, when you measure the distance around a square, you get $s + s + s + s$, or $4s$.

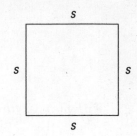

In a rectangle, like all parallelograms, the opposite sides are parallel and congruent. The perimeter of a **rectangle** is $2l + 2w$, where l equals the length and w equals the width. Always remember that the length is longer.

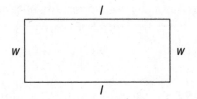

To find the perimeter of a triangle, you just add up the lengths of all three sides:

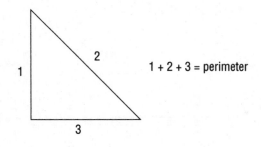

Let's practice!

Find the perimeter of a square whose side is 5 cm.

You know that each side of a square is equal. So, if you know that one side of a square is 5 cm, then you know that each side of the square is 5 cm. To calculate the perimeter, add up the lengths of all four sides.

$$5 + 5 + 5 + 5 = 20$$

So, the perimeter of a square whose side measures 5 cm is 20 cm.

TIP: Be alert when you work with geometry problems to make sure that the units are consistent. If they are different, you must make a conversion before calculating perimeter or area.

PRACTICE

1. Find the perimeter.

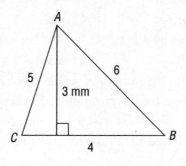

2. Find the perimeter.

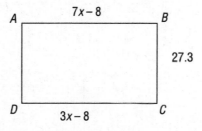

3. Find the perimeter.

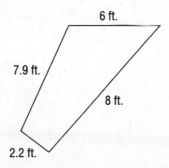

ANSWERS

1. Add up the lengths of all sides, that is, *AB*, *BC*, and *AC*. The height, 3 mm, is information that is not needed to calculate the perimeter. Substitute in to get $6 + 4 + 5 = 15$ millimeters.

2. In a rectangle, like all parallelograms, the opposite sides are parallel and congruent. In this example, $\overline{AB} \cong \overline{DC}$. Use algebra to solve for the variable x.

Set up an equation:	$7x - 4 = 3x + 18$
Subtract $3x$ from both sides:	$7x - 4 - 3x = 3x + 18 - 3x$
Combine like terms:	$4x - 4 = 18$
Add 4 to both sides:	$4x - 4 + 4 = 18 + 4$
Combine like terms:	$4x = 22$
Divide both sides by 4:	$\frac{4x}{4} = \frac{22}{4}$
	$x = 5.5$

   Use this value to find the length of $\overline{AB}$ and $\overline{DC}$: $3x + 18 = (3 \times 5.5) + 18 = 34.5$. Use the shortcut for the perimeter of a rectangle: $P = (2 \times 34.5) + (2 \times 27.3) = 69 + 54.6 = 123.6$ inches.

3. To find perimeter, you add up all the lengths of the sides of the polygon. The perimeter is $7.4 + 6 + 2.2 + 8 = 23.6$ feet.

area

Circles to square and cubes to double
would give a man excessive trouble.
—MATTHEW PRIOR (1664–1721)

This lesson will explore area and how to identify it for common and irregular shaped figures.

AREA IS A measure of how many square units it takes to *cover* a closed figure. Area is measured in square units.

Area is a multiplication concept, where two measures are multiplied together. You can also think of units being multiplied together: $cm \times cm = cm^2$, or the words *centimeters squared*.

When you measured lengths, you used different units, like feet, meters, inches, and so on. When you find the **area**, you use square units.

Here are the area formulas that you should know.

CALCULATING AREA

Figure	Area Calculation	Area Formula
square	side × side	$A = s^2$
	or	or
	base × height	$A = bh$
rectangle	base × height	$A = bh$
parallelogram	base × height	$A = bh$
triangle	$\frac{1}{2}$ × base × height	$A = \frac{1}{2}bh$
trapezoid	$\frac{1}{2}$ × base$_1$ × height + $\frac{1}{2}$ × base$_2$ × height	$A = \frac{1}{2}h(b_1 + b_2)$
circle	π × radius squared	$A = \pi r^2$

When calculating the area of a circle, you will see the π symbol. π, also called pi, is known as a mathematical constant, and represents the number 3.14159. (We often use 3.14.)

Let's try finding the area of the parallelogram.

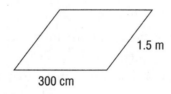

Because the figure is a parallelogram, the height is the length that is perpendicular to the base, not a side of the figure. The base is 300 cm, and the height is 1.5 m. Before using the area formula, all units need to be consistent. Change 300 cm into meters before proceeding. There are 100 centimeters in a meter; therefore, there are 300 divided by 100 meters, which is 3 meters in the base.

Use the area formula and substitute in the given lengths: $A = bh$

Multiply the base times the height: $A = 1.5 \times 3$

$A = 4.5$

Include the square units: $A = 4.5 \text{ m}^2$

PRACTICE

1. Find the area.

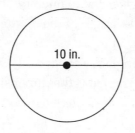

2. Find the area.

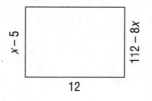

3. Find the area.

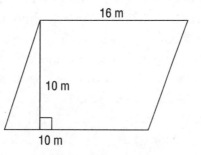

4. Find the area of the irregular figure. Use 3.14 for π.

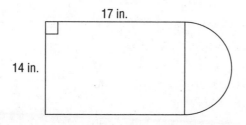

ANSWERS

1. The area of a circle is $A = \pi r^2$, where π is a constant, and r is the radius of the circle. The problem gives the diameter to be 10 in. The radius, 5 inches, is one-half of the length of the diameter. Using the formula $A = \pi \times 5 \times 5$, the area is 25π in^2.

2. Opposite sides of a rectangle are congruent. Use this fact and algebra to solve for the variable x. Then find the dimension's length of the side of the rectangle. Multiply this by the side of length 12 to get the area:

Set up an equation:	$x - 5 = 112 - 8x$
Add $8x$ to both sides:	$x - 5 + 8x = 112 - 8x + 8x$
Combine like terms:	$9x - 5 = 112$
Add 5 to both sides:	$9x - 5 + 5 = 112 + 5$
Combine like terms:	$9x = 117$
Divide both sides by 9:	$\frac{9x}{9} = \frac{117}{9}$
	$x = 13$

   Use this value to find the side of the rectangle: $x - 5 = 13 - 5 = 8$ m. The area is $8 \times 12 = 96$ m^2.

3. The area of a trapezoid is $A = \frac{1}{2}h(b_1 + b_2)$, where A stands for area, b_1 and b_2 are the lengths of the parallel bases, and h is the height, the length of the segment perpendicular to the bases. In this trapezoid, the height = 10 m, because it is perpendicular to the bases. The bases are the parallel sides, 16 m and 10 m. Substitute the given information into the formula: $A = \frac{1}{2} \times 10 \times (16 + 10)$ to get $A = \frac{1}{2} \times 10 \times (26)$. Multiply all terms on the right together to yield an area of 130 m^2.

4. This figure is a rectangle and one-half of a circle. The area will be $A = A_{\text{rectangle}} + (A_{\text{circle}}$ divided by 2): $A = bh + \pi r^2 \div 2$. The radius is one-half of the width of the rectangle; the radius is 7: $A = (14 \times 17) + \frac{(3.14 \times 7^2)}{2} = 238 + 76.93 = 314.93$ in^2.

L E S S O N 21

symmetry and similarity

*Symmetry, as wide or as narrow as you define its meaning,
is one idea by which man through the ages has tried to
comprehend and create order, beauty and perfection.*
—Hermann Weyl (1885–1955)

In this lesson, you will see two different properties of figures—symmetry and
similarity.

SHAPES ARE SAID to be **symmetrical** if you can make a line through that
shape, forming two halves that are mirror images of each other. Look at any figure and see if you can draw an imaginary line, such that if you folded the figure at this line, the figure would fall on top of itself. There can be none, one, or several lines of symmetry for a figure. Two types of symmetry are line symmetry and rotational symmetry.

A figure has **line symmetry** if it can be folded so that one half of the figure coincides with the other half.

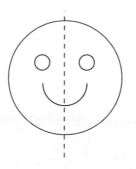

Congruent figures have the same size and shape. All corresponding parts, the sides and angles, have the same measure. They can be moved by a slide, flip, or turn. These movements are called **transformations**.

A **reflection** is where a figure is flipped over the **line of symmetry**, which divides a figure into two identical halves.

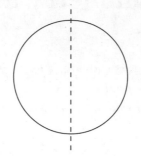

Look at the letter *A*. If you split it in half with a vertical line, you end up with two identical halves.

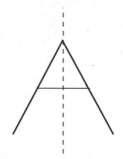

The letter *A* has line symmetry.

Now look at the letter Z. Can you draw a vertical or horizontal line to make two equal sides? No, so you know that the letter Z does not have line symmetry.

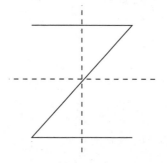

A **rotation** is when something is turned completely around a central point. A figure has **rotational symmetry** if it looks exactly the same after it has been rotated 360 degrees.

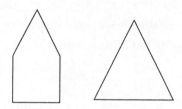

2 Figures with Rotational Symmetry

A **translation** is a slide of a figure that slides every point of the figure the same distance in the same direction.

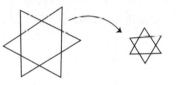

Translation

PRACTICE 1

Look at the letters that follow.

Z	E
S	N
H	C
O	

1. Which letters have line symmetry?

2. Which letters have rotational symmetry?

SIMILAR FIGURES

Two figures are **similar** if they are the same shape but different sizes. The symbol for similarity is ~.

For four-sided figures, this means that corresponding angles are congruent, and corresponding sides are in proportion.

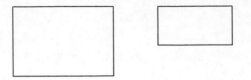

If you are told that two figures are similar, then their corresponding sides are in proportion. If the scale factor is not apparent, set up a proportion. Remember, a proportion is an equation in which two ratios are equal. Proportional problems are solved using cross multiplication.

PRACTICE 2

Determine whether rectangles *ABCD* and *EFGH* are similar.

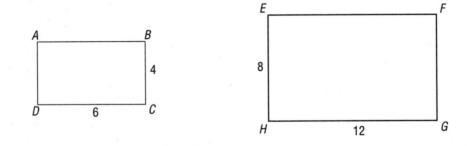

ANSWERS

Practice 1

1. H, O, E, C
2. Z, S, H, O, N

Practice 2

Both are rectangles, so all the angles are equal. You need to determine if the corresponding sides are in proportion. If $ABCD$ and $EFGH$ are similar, then $\frac{AD}{EH}$ will equal $\frac{CD}{GH}$. $AD = 4$ and $EH = 8$. So $\frac{AD}{EH}$ is $\frac{4}{8}$, or $\frac{1}{2}$. $CD = 6$ and $GH = 12$. So $\frac{CD}{GH}$ is $\frac{6}{12}$, or $\frac{1}{2}$. These rectangles are similar.

classifying triangles

The only angle from which to approach
a problem is the TRY-Angle.
—AUTHOR UNKNOWN

The triangle is the fundamental figure in geometry. This lesson will expose the different types of triangles and how to use the Pythagorean theorem.

A TRIANGLE IS a figure with three equal sides. The sum of the measure of the angles in a triangle is equal to 180°.

A triangle can be classified by its angles: acute, right, or obtuse.

Acute triangles have all angles less than 90°.

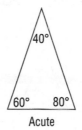

Acute

Equilateral triangles have all angles equal to 60°. All sides of equilateral triangles are congruent (equal).

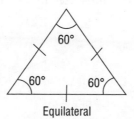

Equilateral

Obtuse triangles have one angle that is greater than 90°.

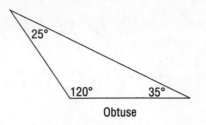

Obtuse

Right triangles have one right (90°) angle.

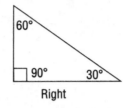

Right

. . . .

TIP: Be careful when you classify triangles by angle measure. Notice that even though right triangles and obtuse triangles each have two acute angles, their classification is not affected by these angles. Acute triangles have all *three* acute angles.

. . . .

A triangle can also be classified by its sides: scalene, isosceles, or equilateral. **Isosceles triangles** have two congruent sides (and the angles opposite these equal sides are equal as well).

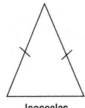

Isosceles

Scalene triangles have no sides that are congruent.

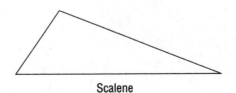

Scalene

PRACTICE 1

1. Which of the terms describes this triangle?

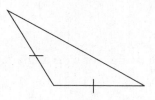

2. Select the right name for the following triangle:

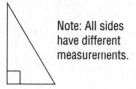

Note: All sides
have different
measurements.

> right isosceles
> acute scalene
> obtuse isosceles
> acute isosceles
> right scalene

CONGRUENT TRIANGLES

Triangles with the same size and shape are **congruent** triangles. The matching parts of congruent triangles are called **congruent parts**.

You can determine that two triangles are congruent if the following corresponding parts are congruent:

3 sides or side-side-side (SSS)

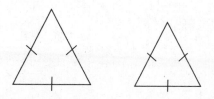

2 angles and the included side or angle-side-angle (ASA)

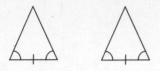

2 sides and the included angle or side-angle-side (SAS)

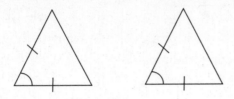

SIMILAR TRIANGLES

Triangles with the same shape, but different sizes, are **similar** triangles. The angles are equal, but the sides vary in length. Similarity is indicated by the ~ symbol.

PRACTICE 2

1. Triangle A has angles measuring 100 degrees, 40 degrees, and a degrees. Triangle B has angles measuring 40 degrees, 30 degrees, and b degrees. Are they similar?

RIGHT TRIANGLES AND THE PYTHAGOREAN THEOREM

Right triangles have one right angle. They are special because you can use the **Pythagorean theorem:**

$$a^2 + b^2 = c^2$$

Here, a and b are the legs of the triangle and c is the hypotenuse. The **hypotenuse** is the side opposite the right angle.

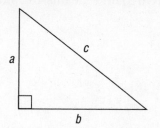

The hypotenuse is equal to the sum of the squares of the lengths of the legs. Let's look at an example. What is the hypotenuse for the following triangle?

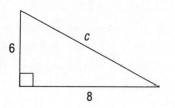

Using the Pythagorean theorem, substitute the values that you know:

$$a^2 + b^2 = c^2$$
$$6^2 + 8^2 = c^2$$
$$36 + 64 = c^2$$
$$100 = c^2$$
$$\sqrt{100} = c^2$$
$$10 = c$$

So, the hypotenuse length is 10. This also means that the lengths 6, 8, and 10 work in a right triangle. Three numbers that prove the Pythagorean theorem are called **Pythagorean triples**. Three other Pythagorean triples include 3-4-5, 5-12-13, and 8-15-17.

PRACTICE 3

Use the Pythagorean theorem to find the missing side.

1.

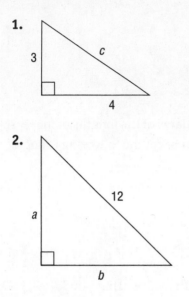

2.

ANSWERS

Practice 1

1. This triangle has an angle greater than 90 degrees, which makes it obtuse. It also has two equal sides, so it is also isosceles. Therefore, it is an obtuse isosceles triangle.
2. The triangle is a right triangle, because it has an angle of 90°, as shown by the small box marked in the angle. The classification by sides is scalene, because all of the side measurements are different. Therefore, it is a right scalene triangle.

Practice 2

1. The sum of the angles in a triangle is 180 degrees.

In triangle A, $110 + 40 + a = 180$. Solving for a, you see that $150 + a = 180$ and $a = 30$.

In triangle B, $40 + 30 + b = 180$. Solving for b, you see that $70 + b = 180$ and $b = 110$.

The angles in triangle A are 110, 40, and 30.

The angles in triangle B are 40, 30, and 110. The angles in both triangles are equal, so they are similar.

Practice 3

1. $a^2 + b^2 = c^2$
$3^2 + 4^2 = c^2$
$9 + 16 = c^2$
$25 = c^2$
$\sqrt{25} = c^2$
$5 = c$

2. $a^2 + b^2 = c^2$
$a^2 + 6^2 = 12^2$
$a^2 + 36 = 144$
$a^2 + 36 - 36 = 144 - 36$
$a^2 = 108$
$\sqrt{a^2} = \sqrt{108}$
$a = \sqrt{108}$

L E S S O N 23

circles and circumference

It is easier to square a circle than to get round a mathematician.
—AUGUSTUS DE MORGAN (1806–1871)

You've undoubtedly come across the circle in your lifetime. But how well do you really know this shape? This lesson will teach you the parts of a circle and expose you to the circle's accomplice—pi.

A CIRCLE IS a closed figure in which each point of the circle is the same distance from the center of the circle.

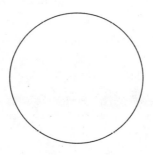

A **chord** is a line segment that joins two points on a circle.

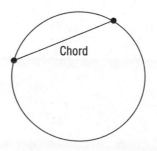

A **radius** is a line segment from the center of the circle to a point on the circle. You can name a radius by its points.

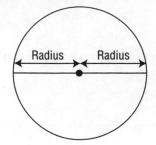

A **diameter** is a chord that passes through the center of the circle and has endpoints on the circle. You can name a diameter by its points.

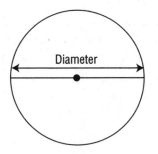

An **arc** is a curved line that makes up part or all of a circle. If a circle is comprised of two arcs, the larger arc is called the **major arc,** and the smaller arc is called the **minor arc.**

A **minor arc** is the smaller curve between two points.

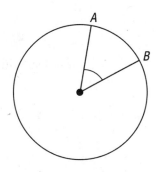

A **major arc** is the larger curve between two points.

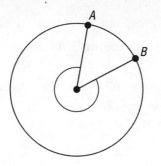

MEASURING A CIRCLE

When you measure the distance around a circle, the distance is called a **circumference**. Think of circumference and circles the same way you think of quadrilaterals and perimeter: They are both measures of the distance around the outside.

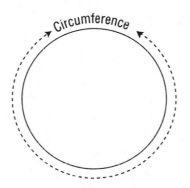

As you learned in Lesson 20, when you deal with circles and circumference, you deal with a circle's partner pi, which is also represented by the symbol π. Pi is the ratio between the circumference of a circle and its diameter. It is equal to about 3.14, or $\frac{22}{7}$.

TIP: On most math tests, you will be advised to use π or one of the approximate values of π: 3.14, or $\frac{22}{7}$. Pay close attention to which one you are told to work with.

For the circumference of a **circle**, C, use one of the following formulas:

$C = 2\pi r$, which translates to pi times twice the radius

$C = \pi d$, which translates to pi times the diameter

Notice that both of these formulas are correct because the diameter is twice the radius. In other words, $2r = d$.

Let's look at an example.

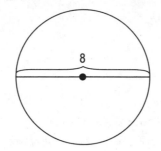

The circumference of this circle is 8π because the diameter is 8.

Try another. But use 3.14 for pi.

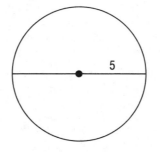

The radius is 5, so plug this into the circumference formula:

$C = 2\pi 5$

You know that 2 times 5 is 10, so you can simplify the expression to 10π. But you haven't finished just yet. You were told to use 3.14 for pi. Plug in that value:

$C = 10\pi$

$C = 10 \times 3.14$

$C = 31.4$

The circumference is 31.4 inches.

PRACTICE

Use the following circle to answer the questions.

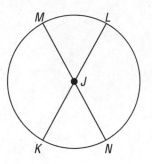

1. Name each radius shown in this circle.

2. Name the diameters shown in this circle.

3. If the length of *MJ* is 15 units, what is the circumference of the circle?

ANSWERS

1. *MJ, LJ, NJ, KJ*
2. *MJN* (or *NJM*) and *KJL* (or *LJK*)
3. The circumference of a circle is equal to 2π*r*, where *r* is the radius of the circle. Therefore, the circumference of this circle is equal to (2π)(15) = 30π units.

three-dimensional figures

One geometry cannot be more true than another,
it can only be more convenient.
—Henri Poincaré (1854–1912)

You have already looked at two-dimensional figures with width and height. Now, you'll look at three-dimensional figures that have a width, height, and depth.

THE WORLD YOU live in is 3-D. When something is three-dimensional, this means that it has depth, width, and height. Look at the objects around you. From your portable Game Boy to your family's car, from a maple tree to lunch, there are many three-dimensional objects that you will cross paths with daily.

A **three-dimensional figure** is a figure that has depth, width, and height. In other words, it is not flat. There are many different types of three-dimensional figures.

Prisms have flat surfaces, called **faces**. The faces meet to form **edges**. The edges meet at corners called **vertices**. (A single corner is called a **vertex**.)

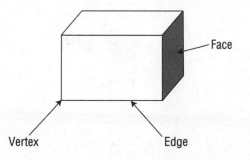

Bases are used to name prisms. For example, a **rectangular solid**, or rectangular prism, is a three-dimensional solid with a rectangle for a base.

Rectangular Solid
(prism)

Think of a rectangular solid as being made of rectangles and squares. It has six faces.

A **cube** is a special type of rectangular solid. In a cube, all the faces are squares.

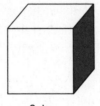

Cube

A **pyramid** has a quadrilateral for a base and triangles for sides. It has four triangular faces sharing a common vertex. In other words, a pyramid always comes to a point. Sometimes, the base is also a triangle, which gives the pyramid four faces.

Pyramid

Like a pyramid, a **cone** is a three-dimensional figure that also comes to a point. It has one circular base and a vertex that is not on the base.

Cone

A **sphere** is one of the most familiar three-dimensional shapes. It has no flat surfaces. You live on Earth—one large sphere! A sphere is made when you twirl a circle around one of its diameters. Like a circle, all the points of a sphere are at the same distance from its center.

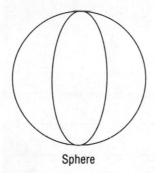

Sphere

A **cylinder** is a three-dimensional figure that has two parallel, congruent bases. Both bases are circles. If you've seen the stockpiles of canned food at a food drive, you've encountered cylinders.

Cylinder

PRACTICE

1. Draw a line from the labels below to their real-world objects.

cone

rectangular prism

cube

cylinder

pyramid

sphere

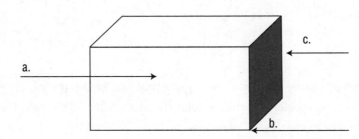

2. Identify the parts labeled in this figure: a., b., and c.

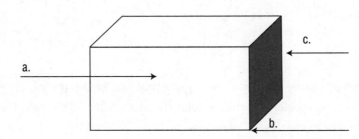

3. How many faces does a cube have?

4. How many vertices does a rectangular prism have?

ANSWERS

1.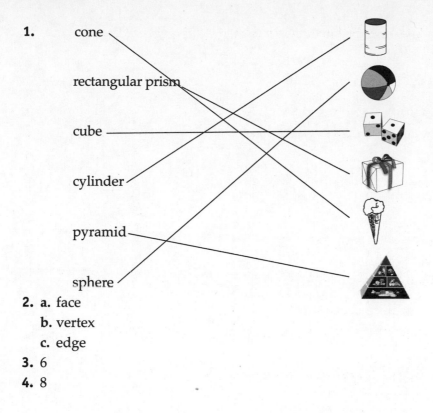

   cone

   rectangular prism

   cube

   cylinder

   pyramid

   sphere

2. a. face
   b. vertex
   c. edge
3. 6
4. 8

LESSON 25

volume of solids

Where there is matter, there is geometry.
—JOHANNES KEPLER (1571–1630)

In this lesson, you'll discover different formulas used to determine volume, or the amount of cubic units needed to fill a three-dimensional solid.

THE VOLUME OF a three-dimensional figure is the amount of space the figure occupies. Volume is always measured in **cubic units**, such as in.^{3} or cm^3.

The volume of a **cylinder** can be found by using the formula:

$V = \pi r^2 h$

In this formula, r is the radius of the cylinder, and h is its height.

Look at the following cylinder.

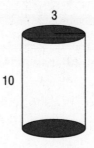

It has a height of 10 units and a radius of 3 units. Substitute these values into the volume formula:

$$V = \pi r^2 h$$
$$V = \pi(3)^2(10)$$
$$V = \pi(9)(10)$$
$$V = 90\pi$$

The volume is 90π cubic units. (Always remember to include the cubic units in your answer!)

....

TIP: Questions that involve glasses usually refer to cylinders.

....

The volume of a rectangular solid uses the following formula:

$$V = lwh$$

In this formula, l is the length of the rectangular solid, w is its width, and h is its height.

Look at the following rectangular solid.

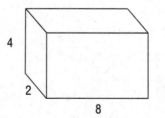

The rectangular solid has a length of 8 units, a width of 2 units, and a height of 4 units. The volume of the rectangular solid is $lwh = (8)(2)(4) = 64$ cubic units.

Even though the volume of a cube can be found using the formula for the volume of a rectangular solid, there is a shortcut for the volume of a cube:

$$V = s^3$$

The volume of a cube can be described as e^3, where e is the length of an edge of the cube. The length, width, and height of a cube are all the same, so multiplying the length, width, and height is the same as cubing any one of those measurements.

PRACTICE

1. A cylinder has a volume of 45π in^3. Which of the following could be the radius and height of the cylinder?
   a. radius = 9 in., height = 5 in.
   b. radius = 3 in., height = 15 in.
   c. radius = 5 in., height = 3 in.
   d. radius = 3 in., height = 5 in.
   e. radius = 9 in., height = 10 in.

2. Terri fills with water $\frac{2}{3}$ of a glass that is 15 cm tall. If the radius of the glass is 2 cm, what volume of water is in Terri's glass?

3. The height of cylinder B is three times the height of cylinder A and the radius of cylinder B is $\frac{1}{3}$ the radius of cylinder A. What is true about the volume of both cylinders?

4. The radius of a cylinder is $2x$ and the height of the cylinder is $8x + 2$. What is the volume of the cylinder in terms of x?

5. The height of a cylinder is four times the radius of the cylinder. If the volume of the cylinder is 256π cm^3, what is the radius of the cylinder?

6. The length of a rectangular solid is twice the sum of the width and height of the rectangular solid. If the width is equal to the height and the volume of the solid is 108 in.^{3}, what is the length of the solid?

7. The area of one face of a cube is $9x$ square units. What is the volume of the cube?

8. The volume of rectangular solid A is equal to the volume of rectangular solid B. If the length of solid A is three times the length of solid B, and the height of solid A is twice the height of solid B, then write a sentence comparing the width of solid B and the width of solid A.

9. The length of a rectangular solid is 6 units and the height of the solid is 12 units. If the volume of the solid is 36 cubic units, what is the width of the solid?

ANSWERS

1. Try each possible combination in the cylinder formula. The volume of a cylinder is equal to $\pi r^2 h$, where r is the radius of the cylinder and h is the height of the cylinder. Only the values of the radius and height given in choice **d** hold true in the formula: $\pi(3)^2(5) = \pi(9)(5) = 45\pi$ in^3.

2. The volume of a cylinder is equal to $\pi r^2 h$, where r is the radius of the cylinder and h is the height of the cylinder. Terri's glass is only $\frac{2}{3}$ full, so the height of the water is $\frac{2}{3}(15) = 10$ cm. Therefore, the volume of water is equal to $\pi(2)^2(10) = 40\pi$ cm^3.

3. The volume of cylinder B is $\frac{1}{3}$ the volume of cylinder A. The volume of a cylinder is equal to $\pi r^2 h$, where r is the radius of the cylinder and h is the height of the cylinder. If the volume of cylinder A is $\pi r^2 h$, then the volume of cylinder B is $\pi(\frac{1}{3}r)^2(3h) = \pi(\frac{1}{9}r^2)(3h) = \pi\frac{1}{3}r^2 h$.

4. The volume of a cylinder is equal to $\pi r^2 h$, where r is the radius of the cylinder and h is the height of the cylinder. The volume of this cylinder is equal to $\pi(2x)^2(8x + 2) = \pi 4x^2(8x + 2) = (32x^3 + 8x^2)\pi$.

5. The volume of a cylinder is equal to $\pi r^2 h$, where r is the radius of the cylinder and h is the height of the cylinder. The height is four times the radius, so the volume of this cylinder is equal to $\pi r^2(4r) = 256\pi$, $4r^3 = 256$, $r^3 = 64$, $r = 4$. The radius of the cylinder is 4 cm.

6. The volume of a rectangular solid is equal to lwh, where l is the length of the solid, w is the width of the solid, and h is the height of the solid. If x represents the width (and therefore, the height as well), then the length of the solid is equal to $2(x + x)$, or $2(2x) = 4x$. Therefore, $(4x)(x)(x) = 108$, $4x^3 = 108$, $x^3 = 27$, and $x = 3$. If the width and height of the solid are each 3 in., then the length of the solid is $2(3 + 3) = 2(6) = 12$ in.

7. One face of a cube is a square. The area of a square is equal to the length of one side of the square multiplied by itself. Therefore, the length of a side of this square (and edge of the cube) is equal to $\sqrt{9x}$, or $3\sqrt{x}$ units. Because every edge of a cube is equal in length and the volume of a cube is equal to e^3, where e is the length of an edge (or lwh, where l is the length of the cube, w is the width of the cube, and h is the height of the cube, which in this case, are all $3\sqrt{x}$ units), the volume of the cube is equal to $(3\sqrt{x})^3 = 27x\sqrt{x}$ cubic units.

8. The width of solid B is six times the width of solid A. The volume of a rectangular solid is equal to lwh, where l is the length of the solid, w is the width of the solid, and h is the height of the solid. If l is the length of solid B and h is the height of solid B, then the length of solid A is $3l$ and the height of solid A is $2h$. Because the volumes of the solids are equal, if w_1 represents the width of solid A and w_2 represents the width of solid B, then $(3l)(2h)(w_1) = (l)(h)(w_2)$, $6w_1 = w_2$, which means that w_2, the width of solid B, is equal to six times the width of solid A.

9. The volume of a rectangular solid is equal to lwh, where l is the length of the solid, w is the width of the solid, and h is the height of the solid. Therefore, $(6)(12)(w) = 36$, $72w = 36$, and $w = \frac{1}{2}$ unit.

surface area of solids

According to most accounts, geometry was first discovered among the Egyptians, taking its origin from the measurement of areas. For they found it necessary by reason of the flooding of the Nile, which wiped out everybody's proper boundaries.

—Proclus (412–485)

In this lesson, you'll practice working with the surface area of a three-dimensional shape, or the sum of the areas of each side of the shape.

THE SURFACE AREA is the area on the surface of a solid figure. Surface area is measured in units^2 (square units).

The formula for the surface area of a cube is:

S.A. = $6(s^2)$

In order to find the surface area of a cube, you would find the area of each face and then find the total of all the faces. Because the area of a square is s^2, you will have six faces with an area of s^2, so in all, you will have $6s^2$.

Look at the following figure.

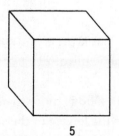

5

The area of one square of the cube is equal to (5)(5) = 25 square units. Because all six squares that comprise the cube are identical, the surface area of the square is equal to (25)(6) = 150 square units.

Here is the formula for the surface area of a rectangular solid:

S.A. = 2(*lw*) + 2(*hw*) + 2(*lh*)

The surface area of a rectangular solid is equal to the sum of the areas of the six rectangles (three pairs of congruent rectangles) that comprise the rectangular solid.

Look at the following figure.

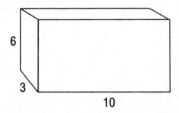

The surface area of the rectangular solid is equal to 2(6 × 10) + 2(6 × 3) + 2(3 × 10) = 2(60) + 2(18) + 2(30) = 120 + 36 + 60 = 216 square units.

PRACTICE

1. A rectangular solid measures 4 units by 5 units by 6 units. What is the surface area of the solid?

2. Danielle's cube has a volume of 512 in³. What is the surface area of her cube?

3. The surface area of a rectangular solid is 192 cm². If the height of the solid is 4 units and the length of the solid is 12 units, what is the width of the solid?

4. The volume of a cube is x^3 cubic units and the surface area of the cube is x^3 square units. What is the value of x?

5. The width of a rectangular solid is twice the height of the solid, and the height of the solid is twice the length of the solid. If x is the length of the solid, what is the surface area of the solid in terms of x?

ANSWERS

1. The surface area of a solid is the sum of the areas of each side of the solid. A rectangular solid has six rectangular faces. Two faces measure 4 units by 5 units, two faces measure 4 units by 6 units, and two faces measure 5 units by 6 units. Therefore, the surface area of the solid is equal to $2(4 \times 5) + 2(4 \times 6) + 2(5 \times 6) = 2(20) + 2(24) + 2(30) = 40 + 48 + 60 = 148$ square units.

2. The volume of a cube is equal to the product of its length, width, and height. The length, width, and height of a cube are identical in measure, so the measure of one edge of Danielle's cube is equal to the cube root of 512, which is equal to 8, because $(8)(8)(8) = 512$. The area of one face of the cube is equal to the product of the length and width of that face. Because every length and width of the cube is 8 units, the area of one face of the cube is $(8)(8) = 64$ square units. A cube has six faces, so the total surface area of the cube is equal to $(64)(6) = 384$ square units.

3. The surface area of a solid is the sum of the areas of each side of the solid. A rectangular solid has six rectangular faces. If w is the width of the solid, then two faces measure 4 units by 12 units, two faces measure 4 units by w units, and two faces measure 12 units by w units. Therefore, the surface area of the solid is equal to $2(4 \times 12) + 2(4 \times w) + 2(12 \times w) = 96 + 8w + 24w = 96 + 32w$. Because the surface area of the solid is 192 cm^2, $96 + 32w = 192$, $32w = 96$, $w = 3$. The width of the solid is 3 units.

4. The volume of a cube is equal to the product of its length, width, and height. The length, width, and height of a cube are identical in measure, so the measure of one edge of the cube is equal to the cube root of x^3, which is equal to x, because $(x)(x)(x) = x^3$. The area of one face of the cube is equal to the product of the length and width of that face. Because every length and width of the cube is x, the area of any one face of the cube is $(x)(x) = x^2$. A cube has six faces, so the total surface area of the cube is equal to $6x^2$ square units. It is given that the surface area of the square is x^3 square units. Therefore, $6x^2 = x^3$. Divide both sides by x^2, and the value of x is 6.

5. The surface area of a solid is the sum of the areas of each side of the solid. A rectangular solid has six rectangular faces. If x is the length of the solid, then $2x$ is the height of the solid and $4x$ is the width of the solid. Two faces of the solid measure x units by $2x$ units, two faces measure x units by $4x$ units, and two faces measure $2x$ units by $4x$ units. Therefore, the surface area of the solid is equal to $2(x \times 2x) + 2(x \times 4x) + 2(2x \times 4x) = 2(2x^2) + 2(4x^2) + 2(8x^2) = 4x^2 + 8x^2 + 16x^2 = 28x^2$.

the coordinate plane

Geometry is just plane fun!
—Author Unknown

This lesson welcomes you into the world of coordinate geometry and teaches you the key terms involved.

IN THE 1600s, René Descartes, a philosopher and mathematician, created a method of positioning a point in a plane by its distance, *x* and *y*, from the intersection of two fixed lines drawn at right angles in the plane. This plane came to be called the Cartesian plane, or simply, the **coordinate plane**.

A coordinate plane is used to plot or locate points in a plane. The horizontal axis is called the *x*-**axis**, and the vertical axis is called the *y*-**axis**.

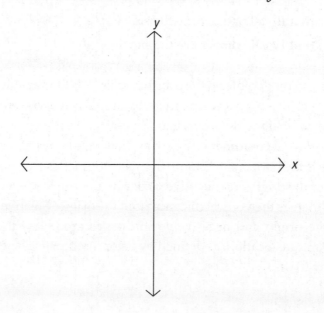

There are four **quadrants** created by the intersection of the x- and y-axes. The quadrants are named by Roman numerals; quadrant I is in the upper right corner. The other quadrants follow in a counterclockwise direction. The intersection of the axes is called the **origin**.

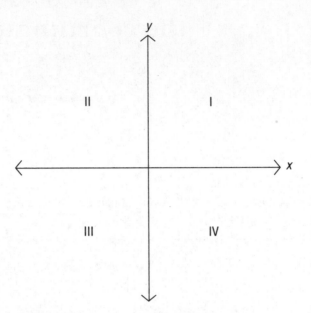

Notice the signs of the ordered pairs and where they lie in the coordinate plane:

In quadrant I, all points have the sign $(+x,+y)$.

In quadrant II, all points have the sign $(-x,+y)$.

In quadrant III, all points have the sign $(-x,-y)$.

In quadrant IV, all points have the sign $(+x,-y)$.

It is easy to plot points on the coordinate grid. Points are given as **ordered pairs**, which are just x/y pairs. An ordered pair is always written (x,y). You simply go left or right along the x-axis to find your x, and then you go up or down to the appropriate y-coordinate. The y-coordinate is always named second. The x-coordinate is the horizontal distance from the origin. Positive x-coordinates are to the right of the origin and negative x-coordinates are to the left of the origin. The y-coordinate is the vertical distance from the origin. Positive y-coordinates are above the origin and negative y-coordinates are below the origin. Each point has a unique location, as defined by its ordered pair. The coordinates for the origin are $(0,0)$.

The following graph is an example of the coordinate plane.

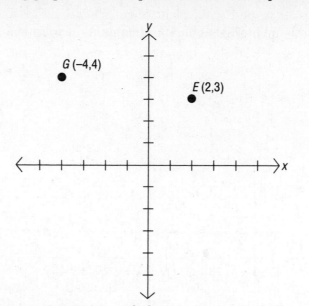

Look at the point labeled *E*, with the coordinates (2,3). The *x*-coordinate is listed first in the coordinate pair. The *x* value of a point is the distance from the *y*-axis to that point. Point *E* is two units from the *y*-axis, so its *x* value is 2. The *y*-coordinate is listed second in the coordinate pair. The *y* value of a point is the distance from the *x*-axis to that point. Point *E* is three units from the *x*-axis, so its *y* value is 3.

What are the coordinates of point *G*? Point *G* is –4 units from the *y*-axis and four units from the *x*-axis. The coordinates of point *G* are (–4,4).

PRACTICE

1. Which points are located at the coordinates in the following chart?

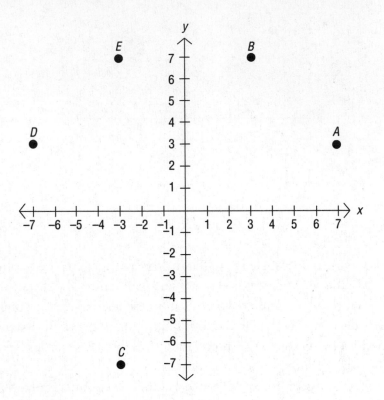

Ordered Pair	Letter
(−3,7)	
(7,3)	
(−3,−7)	
(−7,3)	
(3,7)	

2. Plot the following coordinates on the coordinate plane that follows.

    A: (6,–1)

    B: (–3,–5)

    C: (–2,8)

    D: (1,7)

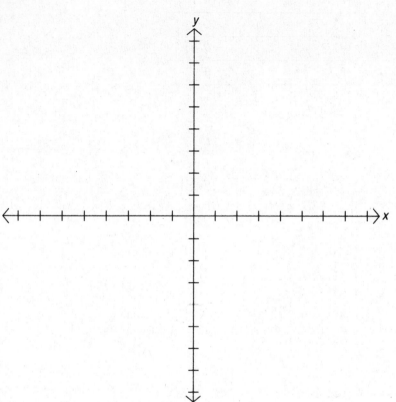

ANSWERS

1.

Ordered Pair	Letter
(−3,7)	E
(7,3)	A
(−3,−7)	C
(−7,3)	D
(3,7)	B

2.

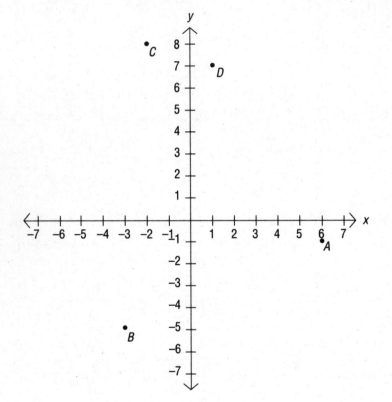

slope of a line

A line is a dot that went for a walk.
—Paul Klee (1879–1940)

Now that you are familiar with the coordinate plane, this lesson takes you a little deeper into the world of coordinate geometry. You will discover slopes, midpoints, and the distance formula.

YOU NOW KNOW how to plot points on a coordinate plane. When two points on the coordinate plane are connected, a line is formed. The **slope** of a line is the difference between the y values of two points divided by the difference between the x values of those two points.

The slope between two points (x_1,y_1) and (x_2,y_2) can be found by using the following formula:

$$\frac{\text{change in } y}{\text{change in } x} = \frac{y_1 - y_2}{x_1 - x_2}$$

Slope is known as "the rise over the run." This means that the number in the numerator (top number) tells how many units to move up or down and the number in the denominator (bottom number) tells how many units to move across to the right or left.

Let's try to find the slope of the line between the points (–2,5) and (3,3).

Use the formula for slope:

$$\frac{y_1 - y_2}{x_1 - x_2}$$
$$= \frac{5 - 3}{-2 - 3}$$
$$= \frac{2}{-5}$$

Here, the slope, or the rise over the run, is $\frac{2}{-5}$. As you learned in Lesson 4, a negative fraction, no matter where the negative sign is placed, makes the entire fraction negative. Therefore, you could also write the slope as $-\frac{2}{5}$.

....

TIP: If both the y value and the x value increase from one point to another, or if both the y value and the x value decrease from one point to another, the slope of the line is positive. If the y value increases and the x value decreases from one point to another, or if the y value decreases and the x value increases from one point to another, the slope of the line is negative.

....

A horizontal line has a slope of 0. Lines such as $y = 9$ or $y = -5$ are lines with slopes of 0.

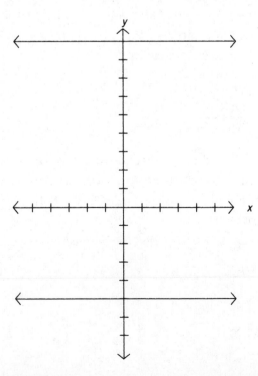

A vertical line has no slope. Lines such as $x = 2$ or $x = -8$ are lines with no slopes.

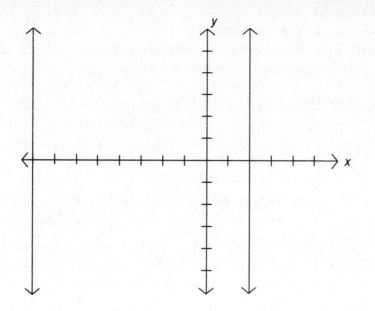

MIDPOINT

Any two points determine a segment on the coordinate plane. Every segment has a **midpoint**. The midpoint is exactly halfway between the two points.

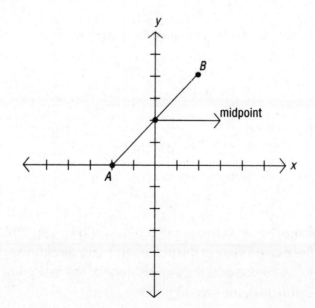

The coordinates of the midpoint of a segment, given the coordinates of its endpoints as (x_1, y_1) and (x_2, y_2), is midpoint = $\left(\dfrac{x_1 + x_2}{2}, \dfrac{y_1 + y_2}{2} \right)$. This is called the **midpoint formula**.

Let's try a midpoint problem.

What is the midpoint of the segment with endpoints A $(-3, -5)$ and B $(-6, 7)$?

Plug the numbers into the midpoint formula.

$$M = \left(\frac{-3 + -6}{2}, \frac{-5 + 7}{2} \right)$$
$$= \left(\frac{-9}{2}, \frac{2}{2} \right)$$
$$= (-4.5, 1)$$

You can also use the midpoint formula to find a missing coordinate.

What is the endpoint, C, of a segment whose midpoint, M, is $(7, 0)$ and other endpoint is D $(10, 4)$?

Use the midpoint formula to find (x_2, y_2):

$$\frac{10 + x_2}{2} = 7$$
$$\frac{4 + y_2}{2} = 0$$

Multiply both sides by 2:

$$10 + x_2 = 14$$
$$4 + y_2 = 0$$

Now, subtract from both sides to isolate the variable:

$$x_2 = 4$$
$$y_2 = -4$$

The other endpoint is $(4, -4)$.

DISTANCE

To find the **distance** between two points, use the following formula. The variable x_1 represents the x-coordinate of the first point, x_2 represents the x-coordinate of the second point, y_1 represents the y-coordinate of the first point, and y_2 represents the y-coordinate of the second point:

$$D = \sqrt{(x_2 - x_1)^2 + (y_2 - y_1)^2}$$

What is the distance between the points (–2,8) and (4,–2)?

Substitute these values into the formula:

$$D = \sqrt{(4 - (-2))^2 + ((-2) - 8)^2}$$
$$D = \sqrt{(4 + 2)^2 + (-2 - 8)^2}$$
$$D = \sqrt{(6)^2 + (-10)^2}$$
$$D = \sqrt{36 + 100}$$
$$D = \sqrt{136}$$
$$D = 2\sqrt{34}$$

PRACTICE

1. The endpoints of a line segment are (–3,6) and (7,4). What is the slope of this line?

2. The endpoints of a line segment are (5,–5) and (–5,–5). What is the slope of this line?

3. What is the slope of a line segment with endpoints at (–1,2) and (1,10)?

4. What is the midpoint of a line segment with endpoints at (0,–8) and (–8,0)?

5. What is the midpoint of a line segment with endpoints at (6,–4) and (15,8)?

6. The endpoints of a line segment are (0,–4) and (0,4). What is the midpoint of this line?

7. What is the distance from the point (–6,2) to the point (2,17)?

8. What is the distance from the point (0,–4) to the point (4,4)?

9. What is the distance from the point (3,8) to the point (7,–6)?

ANSWERS

1. The slope of a line is the difference between the y values of two points divided by the difference between the x values of those two points: $\frac{4-6}{7-(-3)} = \frac{-2}{10} = \frac{-1}{5}$.

2. The slope of a line is the difference between the y values of two points divided by the difference between the x values of those two points: $\frac{-5-(-5)}{5-(-5)} = \frac{0}{10} = 0$.

3. The slope of a line is the difference between the y values of two points divided by the difference between the x values of those two points: $\frac{10-2}{1-(-1)} = \frac{8}{2} = 4$.

4. The midpoint of a line segment is equal to the average of the x values of the endpoints and the average of the y values of the endpoints: $\left(\frac{0+(-8)}{2}, \frac{-8+0}{2}\right) = \left(\frac{-8}{2}, \frac{-8}{2}\right) = (-4,-4)$.

5. The midpoint of a line segment is equal to the average of the x values of the endpoints and the average of the y values of the endpoints: $\left(\frac{6+15}{2}, \frac{-4+8}{2}\right) = \left(\frac{21}{2}, \frac{4}{2}\right) = (10.5,2)$.

6. The midpoint of a line is equal to the average of the x values of the endpoints and the average of the y values of the endpoints: $\left(\frac{0+0}{2}, \frac{-4+4}{2}\right) = \left(\frac{0}{2}, \frac{0}{2}\right) = (0,0)$.

7. To find the distance between two points, use the distance formula:
$$D = \sqrt{(x_2 - x_1)^2 + (y_2 - y_1)^2}$$
$$D = \sqrt{(2 - (-6))^2 + (17 - 2)^2}$$
$$D = \sqrt{8^2 + (15)^2}$$
$$D = \sqrt{64 + 225}$$
$$D = \sqrt{289} = 17 \text{ units}$$

8. To find the distance between two points, use the distance formula:
$$D = \sqrt{(x_2 - x_1)^2 + (y_2 - y_1)^2}$$
$$D = \sqrt{(4 - 0)^2 + (4 - (-4))^2}$$
$$D = \sqrt{4^2 + 8^2}$$
$$D = \sqrt{16 + 64}$$
$$D = \sqrt{80} = \sqrt{16} \times \sqrt{5} = 4\sqrt{5} \text{ units}$$

9. To find the distance between two points, use the distance formula:
$$D = \sqrt{(x_2 - x_1)^2 + (y_2 - y_1)^2}$$
$$D = \sqrt{(7 - 3)^2 + ((-6) - 8)^2}$$
$$D = \sqrt{4^2 + (-14)^2}$$
$$D = \sqrt{16 + 196}$$
$$D = \sqrt{212} = \sqrt{4} \times \sqrt{53} = 2\sqrt{53} \text{ units}$$

● P ● O ● S ● T ● T ● E ● S ● T ●

THIS POSTTEST HAS 30 multiple-choice questions about topics that you've studied in these 28 lessons. Use this posttest to determine any areas you may need to review again.

Read each question carefully. Circle your answers if the book belongs to you. If it doesn't, write the numbers 1–30 on a paper and write your answers there. Try not to use a calculator. Instead, work out each problem on paper.

When you finish the test, check the answers on page 213.

POSTTEST

1. Hector has 93 carrots he wants to share evenly among 31 rabbits. Which of the following number sentences could be used to find the number of carrots each rabbit receives?
   a. $93 \div 31$
   b. $93 - 31$
   c. 93×31
   d. $31 \div 93$

2. A rack designed to hold DVDs has five shelves. Each shelf can hold up to 50 DVDs. What is the maximum number of DVDs that the rack can hold?
   a. 500
   b. 250
   c. 200
   d. 55

3. $|-8 \times 4| + |-5| =$
   a. -37
   b. -27
   c. 27
   d. 37

4. Evaluate: $10 \times (4 - 1 \div 2)$
   a. 15
   b. 19
   c. 35
   d. 39.5

5. Terri's favorite number is 8. She makes a list of multiples of 8. Which number could NOT be on the list?
   a. 4
   b. 8
   c. 56
   d. 8,000

6. Tammy, Elena, Nicole, and Melanie each find a seashell on the beach. Tammy's seashell weighs $\frac{5}{6}$ pounds, Elena's seashell weighs 0.68 pounds, Nicole's seashell weighs 0.8 pounds, and Melanie's seashell weighs $\frac{7}{10}$ pounds. Whose seashell is the heaviest?
  a. Tammy's seashell
  b. Elena's seashell
  c. Nicole's seashell
  d. Melanie's seashell

7. Cecil lives $1\frac{5}{8}$ miles from his school. Which of the following decimals is equal to the distance from Cecil's home to his school?
  a. 0.625 miles
  b. 1.58 miles
  c. 1.125 miles
  d. 1.625 miles

8. Reggie plans to have a garden with 36 plants. He wants the ratio of tomato plants to cucumber plants to be 4:5. How many cucumber plants will be in Reggie's garden?
  a. 5 cucumber plants
  b. 16 cucumber plants
  c. 18 cucumber plants
  d. 20 cucumber plants

9. There are 360 exhibits at the Kendall County Art Fair; 54 of the exhibits are outdoors and the rest are indoors. What percent of the exhibits are outdoors?
  a. 7%
  b. 15%
  c. 18%
  d. 54%

10. The manager of a supermarket wants to figure out which type of bread is most popular with her customers. To make it easier to keep track of the kinds of bread she sells, she numbers the different breads as follows: 1 for white bread, 2 for whole wheat, 3 for rye, and so on. Then she keeps track of breads as they are sold, making a list of all the numbers. To determine which type of bread is the most popular, what information should she look at from this set of data?
a. the mean
b. the median
c. the mode
d. the range

11. Dexter's sixth-grade class races model cars and the results of the race are shown in the following table.

CAR	PLACE	AVERAGE SPEED	TOP SPEED
Firebird	1st	7 mph	9 mph
Thunder	2nd	6 mph	10 mph
Blue Smoke	3rd	6 mph	8 mph
Rally	4th	5 mph	9 mph
Flash	5th	4 mph	12 mph

Which of the following is a valid conclusion?
a. Cars with faster average speeds place higher than cars with slower average speeds.
b. Cars with higher top speeds place higher than cars with lower top speeds.
c. The average speed of a car is not related to the place in which the car finishes.
d. The lower the average speed of a car, the lower the top speed of the car.

12. Four friends study the equation $y = 8x - 10$ and each makes a statement. Which of the following statements is correct?
a. Mike: $y = 0$ when $x = 0$
b. David: $y = 6$ when $x = 2$
c. Frank: $y = 0$ when $x = -2$
d. Dan: $y = 2$ when $x = 1$

13. Susie wants to find the value of $y = 7x - 2$ when $x = 5$. She solves the equation and finds y to be equal to 25. What did Susie do wrong?
  a. She substituted 5 for x and multiplied by 7 before subtracting 2.
  b. She substituted 4 for x and multiplied by 7 before subtracting 2.
  c. She subtracted 2 from 7 before substituting 5 for x and multiplying.
  d. She subtracted 2 from x before substituting and multiplying.

14. The local city council has decided to limit the heights of the buildings in the city to 45 feet so that everybody has a reasonable view of the mountains in the distance. The council has also decided that structures that are eight feet tall or less do not classify as buildings under the city's building code. If H represents the height of a building in feet, which inequality describes the possible range of eligible heights of buildings in this city?
  a. $8 \leq H \leq 45$
  b. $8 \leq H < 45$
  c. $8 < H \leq 45$
  d. $8 < H < 45$

15. Calculate $43^2 \times 4$.
  a. 172
  b. 129
  c. 7,396
  d. 1,849

16. Evaluate the following expression and express the answer in scientific notation.
$$(4 \times 10^2) \times (2 \times 10^3)$$
  a. 8×10^6
  b. 8×10^5
  c. 800×10^3
  d. 800,000

17. What is another way to write $5\sqrt{12}$?
  a. $12\sqrt{5}$
  b. $10\sqrt{3}$
  c. $6\sqrt{3}$
  d. 12

18. Max, David, and Jonathan collect sweaters for a clothing drive. Max collects 57 sweaters, David collects 98 sweaters, and Jonathan collects 72 sweaters. To find the total number of sweaters collected, the boys could use any of the following formulas EXCEPT
   a. 57 + (98 + 72)
   b. 57(98 + 72)
   c. (57 + 98) + 72
   d. (57 + 72) + 98

19. The sum of the measures of two angles is 90°. The angles must be
   a. complementary.
   b. supplementary.
   c. congruent.
   d. obtuse.

20. Albert has four line segments. Two line segments are 5 cm long, and two line segments are 7 cm long. Using the four line segments, Albert could construct all of the following EXCEPT a
   a. rectangle.
   b. parallelogram.
   c. rhombus.
   d. quadrilateral.

21. What is the perimeter of an equilateral triangle whose sides are each 5 feet?
   a. 5 feet
   b. 10 feet
   c. 15 feet
   d. 20 feet

22. A rectangle has sides that are 3 feet long and 7 feet wide. What is the area, in square feet, of the rectangle?
   a. 10 square feet
   b. 20 square feet
   c. 21 square feet
   d. 100 square feet

23. Which of the following statements about a figure and its transformation is NOT true?
  a. A translation of a figure is always congruent to the original figure.
  b. A rotation of a figure is always congruent to the original figure.
  c. A reflection of a figure is always congruent to the original figure.
  d. A dilation of a figure is always congruent to the original figure.

24. In a given triangle, the base is b and the height to that base is h. What is the area, A, of the triangle, in terms of b and h?
  a. $A = b + h$
  b. $A = bh$
  c. $A = \frac{1}{2}bh$
  d. $A = 2b + 2h$

25. What is the circumference of a circle of radius 3 meters? Use the approximation 3.14 for π and round your answer to the nearest tenth.
  a. 1.88 meters
  b. 9.4 meters
  c. 18 meters
  d. 18.8 meters

26. Randy builds a three-dimensional figure using paper and scissors. He uses one sheet of paper for each face of his figure. He wants to use as few pieces of paper as possible, so he builds a
  a. cone.
  b. cube.
  c. triangular pyramid.
  d. cylinder.

27. A cube has side lengths of 3 centimeters. What is its volume?
  a. 3 cm^3
  b. 9 cm^3
  c. 18 cm^3
  d. 27 cm^3

28. A cylinder has a height of 12 inches and a base with a diameter of 6 inches. What is the surface area of the cylinder?
  a. 18π square inches
  b. 72π square inches
  c. 81π square inches
  d. 90π square inches

29. Which point lies in quadrant III?
   a. (1,2)
   b. (−1,2)
   c. (1,−2)
   d. (−1,−2)

30. Tabitha draws the line segment shown on the following graph. Which of the statements that follows is true?

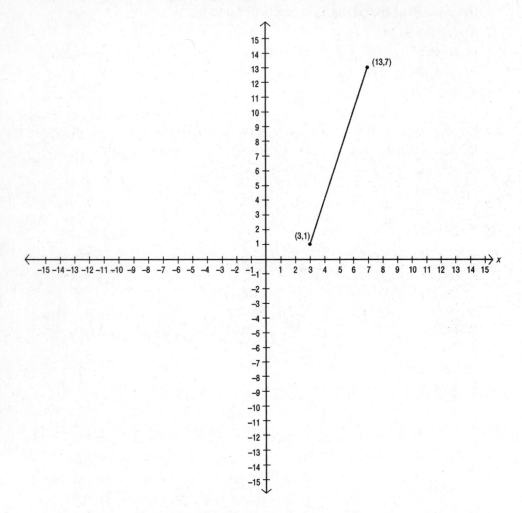

   a. The slope of Tabitha's line segment is $\frac{1}{3}$.
   b. The length of Tabitha's line segment is 12 units.
   c. Tabitha's line segment passes through the point (1,3).
   d. Tabitha's line segment has its midpoint at (5,7).

ANSWERS

1. a. Hector wants to share the carrots among all the rabbits. The key words in this question are *share* and *each*—the word *share* signals division, as does the word *each*. To find the number of carrots each rabbit receives, divide the number of carrots by the number of rabbits:

$$93 \div 31$$

2. b. Each of the five shelves can hold up to 50 DVDs. Therefore, the total number of DVDs the rack can hold is 5×50 DVDs per shelf, or 250 DVDs.

3. d. $-8 \times 4 = -32$, and the absolute value of -32 is 32. The absolute value of -5 is 5; $32 + 5 = 37$.

4. c. Pay close attention to the proper order of operations to evaluate the expression. Start by working inside the parentheses and divide. Then, simplify the difference in the parentheses and multiply. Here are the steps in the evaluation:

$$10 \times (4 - 1 \div 2)$$
$$= 10 \times (4 - 0.5)$$
$$= 10 \times 3.5$$
$$= 35$$

5. a. A multiple of 8 is any number that is divisible by 8. Any number that is less than 8 cannot by divisible by 8. Because 4 is less than 8 and is not divisible by 8, it is the correct answer.

6. a. Convert all four weights to decimals to make them easier to compare. Tammy's seashell weighs $\frac{5}{6}$ pounds. Divide 5 by 6 to convert $\frac{5}{6}$ to a decimal:

$$5 \div 6 = 0.8\overline{3}$$

Convert $\frac{7}{10}$ to a decimal by dividing 7 by 10:

$$7 \div 10 = 0.7$$

Now compare the four decimals. All the weights have a "0" in the ones place. Next, look at the tenths place. Two decimals have an "8" in the tenths place. Nicole's seashell weighs 0.8 pounds, while Tammy's seashell weighs $0.8\overline{3}$ pounds; $0.8\overline{3}$ is greater than 0.8, so Tammy's seashell is the heaviest seashell. Choice **a** is the correct answer.

Nicole's seashell is the next heaviest, followed by Melanie's seashell, and finally, Elena's seashell.

7. d. Convert the fraction $\frac{5}{8}$ to a decimal by dividing 5 by 8:

$$5 \div 8 = 0.625$$

Cecil lives 1 and $\frac{5}{8}$ miles from school, so place a "1" in the ones place of the decimal: 1.625, choice **d**.

8. d. The ratio of tomato plants to cucumber plants is 4:5, which means that 4 out of every 9 plants are tomato plants, and 5 out of every 9 plants are cucumber plants. If $\frac{5}{9}$ of the plants are cucumber plants, and there are 36 total plants, set up a proportion to find the number of cucumber plants:

$$\frac{5}{9} = \frac{x}{36}$$

Cross multiply:

$$9x = 180$$

Divide both sides by 9:

$$x = 20$$

Reggie will have 20 cucumber plants in his garden, choice **d**.

9. b. The question states that 54 out of 360 exhibits are outdoors. To find the percent of outdoor exhibits, divide 54 by 360:

$$54 \div 360 = 0.15$$

0.15 is equal to 15%, choice **b**.

10. c. The mode is the number that occurs most often in a set of data. In these data, the mode would indicate which type of bread sold the most. Choices **a**, **b**, and **d** are not correct because the mean, median, and range do not have any meaning in this problem. The numbers that the manager assigned to each type of bread are not important. For example, she could have used the number 2 for white bread and the number 1 for whole-wheat bread, or used the number 10 or 1,000 for raisin bread. These numbers are identifiers for each type of bread, not actual data values, so calculations based on these values will not be informative.

11. a. Study the table to find relationships between the data in each column.

The cars are listed in the order they placed—1st, 2nd, 3rd, 4th, 5th. Notice that the cars are also in the order of their average speeds—the car that finished first has the fastest average speed, and so on down to the last car, which had the slowest average speed. The conclusion in choice **a**, "Cars with faster average speeds place higher than cars with slower average speeds," is correct.

12. b. For each answer choice, plug the x value into the equation to find the y value.

When $x = 0$:

$y = 8(0) - 10 = -10$, not 0, as Mike incorrectly states in choice **a**.

When $x = 2$:

$y = 8(2) - 10 = 6$, which David correctly states in choice **b**.

When $x = -2$:

$y = 8(-2) - 10 = -26$, not 0, as Frank incorrectly states in choice **c**.

When $x = 1$:

$y = 8(1) - 10 = -2$, not 2, as Dan incorrectly states in choice **d**.

13. c. When you solve an equation, first substitute any variables with their values, and then follow the order of operations: Always perform multiplication and division before addition and subtraction.

Susie subtracted before multiplying. She subtracted 2 from 7 and arrived at 5, and then she multiplied 5 by the value of x, 5, to arrive at 25.

14. c. To be classified as a building, a structure must be more than eight feet tall. This can be represented algebraically as $H > 8$. On the other hand, the height of buildings must not exceed 45 feet. This means that H must be less than or equal to 45, which can be written algebraically as $H \leq 45$. Therefore, the inequality in choice **c** represents the eligible heights in the new building code.

15. c. When any number is squared, that means you are multiplying it by itself: $43 \times 43 = 1,849$. Then it is the simple matter of multiplying that answer by 4: $1,849 \times 4 = 7,396$.

16. b. To evaluate this expression, use the commutative and associative properties of multiplication to rewrite the expression as shown below:
$$(4 \times 10^2) \times (2 \times 10^3) = (4 \times 2) \times (10^2 \times 10^3)$$
Then apply the law of exponents to simplify the expression. Because the bases are the same, you can add the exponents:
$$(4 \times 2) \times (10^2 \times 10^3) = 8 \times 10^{2+3} = 8 \times 10^5$$
This number is in scientific notation, so the answer is **b**.

17. b. $\sqrt{12}$ is the same as $\sqrt{4} \times \sqrt{3}$. The square root of 4 is 2. So $5 \times \sqrt{12}$ is the same as $5 \times 2 \times \sqrt{3}$, which equals $10\sqrt{3}$. Remember, square roots can be multiplied or divided, but they cannot be added or subtracted.

18. b. Choices **a**, **c**, and **d** all show the number of sweaters collected by each boy added together. This is an example of the associative property of addition. When adding three numbers together, the numbers can be added in any order: 58 can be added to the sum of 98 and 72, as in choice **a**; 72 can be added to the sum of 57 and 98, as in choice **c**: or 98 can be added to the sum of 57 and 72, as in choice **d**.

Only choice **b** is NOT true—you cannot multiply the sum of the second and third numbers, 98 and 72, by the first number, 57.

19. a. Two angles are always complementary angles if the sum of their degree measurements equals 90°.

20. c. A rhombus is a four-sided figure with four congruent sides. Albert's four line segments are not the same length, so he cannot construct a rhombus.

21. c. An equilateral triangle has three sides that are all the same length. Therefore, the perimeter is 3×5 ft., or 15 ft.

22. c. The area of a rectangle is its length times its width. Because 3×7 is 21, the answer is 21 square feet.

23. d. A dilation of a figure either enlarges the figure or shrinks it. Therefore, its size changes, and the two figures are not congruent, because congruent figures must have the same size as well as shape.

24. c. To find the area of a triangle, use the formula $A = \frac{1}{2}bh$, where b is the base and h is the height to that base.

25. d. The circumference (C) of the circle in meters is calculated as follows:

$$C = 2\pi r$$
$$= 2(3.14)(3)$$
$$= 18.84$$
$$\approx 18.8$$

So, the circumference of a circle with radius 3 meters is about 18.8 meters.

26. a. Every face of Randy's three-dimensional figure requires one piece of paper. This question is asking you to find the three-dimensional figure with the fewest number of faces. A cone has only two faces, a base, and the body of the cone. A sphere is the only three-dimensional figure with fewer faces (one), but it is not a choice, so a cone, choice **a**, is the correct answer.

27. d. The volume of a cube is side $\times$ side $\times$ side:

$$3 \times 3 \times 3 = 27$$

28. d. Find the surface area of a cylinder by finding the area of its two bases and the area of the curved surface (which, if you flattened it out, would form a rectangle). The base of the cylinder has a radius of 3 inches, so the area of one base is 9π square inches, and the area of both bases is 18π square inches. The area of the curved surface is $12 \times 6\pi$ inches (12 is the height of the cylinder and 6π is the circumference of the circular base), or 72π square inches. Thus, the surface area is $72\pi + 18\pi$, which equals 90π square inches.

29. d. In quadrant III, both the x- and y-coordinates are negative. Choice **a** describes a coordinate in quadrant I. Choice **b** describes a coordinate in quadrant II. Choice **c** describes a coordinate in quadrant IV.

30. d. Read each of the choices and test the statements to see if they are correct.

Choice **a** is incorrect. This slope of Tabitha's line segment can be found by looking at two points on the line segment and dividing the difference between the y-coordinates by the difference between the x-coordinates. The line segment begins at the point (3,1) and ends at the point (7,13).

The slope of the line segment $= \dfrac{y_2 - y_1}{x_2 - x_1}$

The slope of the line segment $= \dfrac{13-1}{7-3}$

The slope of the line segment $= \dfrac{12}{4}$

The slope of the line segment $= 3$

The slope of Tabitha's line segment is 3, not $\frac{1}{3}$.

Choice **b** is also wrong. The distance formula is equal to:

Distance $= \sqrt{(x_2 - x_1)^2 + (y_2 - y_1)^2}$

The length of Tabitha's line segment is equal to:

$\sqrt{(7-3)^2 + (13-1)^2}$

$\sqrt{(4)^2 + (12)^2}$

$\sqrt{16 + 144}$

$\sqrt{160}$, or $4\sqrt{10}$

The length of Tabitha's line segment is $4\sqrt{10}$ units, not 12 units.

Tabitha's line segment does not pass through the point (1,3)—although it does pass through the point (3,1)—so choice **c** is not correct.

The midpoint of a line segment is the point that is halfway between the two endpoints of the line segment. The midpoint can be found by taking the average of the x-coordinates and the average of the y-coordinates of the endpoints:

$\dfrac{x_1 + x_2}{2} = \dfrac{3+7}{2} = \dfrac{10}{2} = 5$

$\dfrac{y_1 + y_2}{2} = \dfrac{1+13}{2} = \dfrac{14}{2} = 7$

The midpoint of Tabitha's line segment is (5,7); therefore, choice **d** is correct.

hints for taking standardized tests

THE TERM *standardized test* has the ability to produce fear in test takers. These tests are often given by a state board of education or a nationally recognized education group. Usually these tests are taken in the hope of getting accepted— whether it's for a special program, the next grade in school, or even to a college or university. Here's the good news: Standardized tests are more familiar to you than you know. In most cases, these tests look very similar to tests that your teachers may have given in the classroom. For most math standardized tests, you may come across two types of questions: multiple-choice and free-response questions. There are some practical ways to tackle both types!

TECHNIQUES FOR MULTIPLE-CHOICE QUESTIONS

The Process of Elimination

For some standardized tests, there is no guessing penalty. What this means is that you shouldn't be afraid to guess. For a multiple-choice question with four answer choices, you have a one in four chance of guessing correctly. And your chances improve if you can eliminate a choice or two.

By using the process of elimination, you will cross out incorrect answer choices and improve your odds of finding the correct answer. In order for the process of elimination to work, you must keep track of what choices you are crossing out. Cross out incorrect choices on the test booklet itself. If you don't cross out an incorrect answer, you may still think it is a possible answer. Crossing out any incorrect answers makes it easier to identify the right answer; there will be fewer places where it can hide!

Don't Supersize

Some multiple-choice questions are long word problems. You may get easily confused if you try to solve the word problems at once. Take bite-sized pieces. Read each sentence one at a time. As soon as you can solve one piece of the problem, go ahead and solve it. Then add on the next piece of information and solve this. Keep adding the information, until you have the final answer. For example:

> Joyce gets $5 for an allowance every day from Monday to Friday. She gets $8 every Saturday and Sunday. If she saves all her allowance for six weeks to buy a new bike, how much will she have?
> a. $150
> b. $240
> c. $246
> d. $254

Take bite-sized pieces of this problem. If Joyce makes $5 every day during the week, she makes $25 a week. If she makes $8 each weekend day, then that is another $16. Joyce makes a total of $41 a week.

Look at the final sentence. If she saves all her allowance for six weeks, you need to calculate 6 times 41, which is $246. There's your answer—choice c!

Use the Answer Choices as Your Tools

You are usually given four choices, one of which is correct. So, if you get stuck, try using the answer choices to jump-start your brain.

Instead of setting up an equation, plug an answer from the answer choices into the problem and see if it works. If it doesn't work, cross out that choice and move on to the next. You can often find the correct answer by trying just one or two of the answer choices!

TECHNIQUES FOR FREE-RESPONSE QUESTIONS

Show Your Work!

Make sure you show all your work. This is good for two reasons. First, some tests that use free-response math questions give you partial credit, even if your final answer is incorrect. If scorers see that you were using the right process to find an answer, you may get some credit. Second, by showing all your work, it is easier for you to review your answer by tracing back all the steps. This can help you cross out any careless calculations or silly mistakes.

TECHNIQUES FOR ALL QUESTIONS

Get Out of Your Head

Use any space in your test booklet to do your math work. When you attempt to do math in your head—even simple arithmetic—you run the chance of making a careless error. Accuracy is more important than speed, so always do your work on paper.

Understand the Question

You need to really get what a question is asking for. Let's say a problem asks you to find the value of $x + 2$. If you don't read carefully, you may solve for x correctly and assume the value of x is your answer. By not understanding what the question was asking for, you have picked the wrong answer.

Skipping Around

You may come across a question that you're not sure how to answer. In these cases, it's okay to skip the question and come back to it later. If your standardized test is timed, you don't want to waste too much time with a troublesome problem. The time might be over before you can get to questions that you would normally whiz through.

If you hit a tricky question, fold down the corner of the test booklet as a reminder to come back to that page later. When you go back to that question with a fresh eye, you may have a better chance of selecting the correct answer.

G L O S S A R Y

absolute value   the distance a number or expression is from zero on a number line

acute angle   an angle that measures less than 90 degrees

acute triangle   a triangle with every angle that measures less than 90 degrees

addend   any number to be added

angle   two rays connected by a vertex

arc   a curved section of a circle

area   a measure of how many square units it takes to cover a closed figure

associative law of addition   the property of numbers that allows you to regroup numbers when you add; for example, $a + (b + c) = (a + b) + c = (a + c) + b$

bar graph   graphic organizer that uses different colored bars that allow for a side-by-side comparison of similar statistics

base   a number used as a repeated factor in an exponential expression

chord   a line segment that goes through a circle with its endpoints on the circle

circle   the set of all points equidistant from one given point, called the *center*. The center point defines the circle, but it is not on the circle.

circumference   the distance around a circle

coefficient   the number placed next to a variable in a term

commutative property of addition   the property of numbers that states that order does not matter when you add; that is, $a + b = b + a$

complementary angles   two angles whose sum is 90 degrees

compound inequality   a combination of two or more inequalities

congruent   identical in shape and size

coordinate plane   a grid divided into four quadrants by both a horizontal x-axis and a vertical y-axis

cross product   a product of the numerator of one fraction and the denominator of a second fraction

decimal   numbers related to or based on the number 10. The place value system is a decimal system because the place values (units, tens, hundreds, etc.) are based on 10.

denominator   the bottom number in a fraction. *Example:* 2 is the denominator in $\frac{1}{2}$.

diameter   a line segment that passes through the center of the circle whose endpoints are on the circle

difference   The difference between two numbers means subtract one number from the other.

distributive property   When you multiply a sum or a difference by a third number, you can multiply each of the first two numbers by the third number and then add or subtract the products.

dividend   a number that is divided by another number

divisible by   A number is divisible by a second number if that second number divides *evenly* into the original number. *Example:* 10 is divisible by 5 ($10 \div 5 = 2$, with no remainder). However, 10 is not divisible by 3.

divisor   a number that is divided into another number

equation   a mathematical statement that can use numbers, variables, or a combination of the two and an equal sign

equilateral triangle   a triangle with three equal sides and three equal angles

even integer   integers that are divisible by 2, such as –4, –2, 0, 2, 4, and so on

exponent   a number that tells you how many times a number, the base, is a factor in the product

expression   a mathematical statement without an equal sign that can use numbers, variables, or a combination of the two

factor   a number that is multiplied to find a product

fraction   the result of dividing two numbers. When you divide 3 by 5, you get $\frac{3}{5}$, which equals 0.6. A fraction is a way of expressing a number that involves dividing a top number (the numerator) by a bottom number (the denominator).

greatest common factor   the largest of all the common factors of two or more numbers

hypotenuse   the longest leg of a right triangle always opposite the right angle

improper fraction   a fraction whose numerator is greater than or equal to its denominator

inequality   sentences that compare quantities that are greater than, less than, greater than or equal to, or less than or equal to symbols

integer   a number along the number line, such as –3, –2, –1, 0, 1, 2, 3, and so on. Integers include whole numbers and their negatives.

isosceles triangle   a triangle with two equal sides

least common denominator   the smallest number divisible by two or more denominators

least common multiple   the smallest of all the common multiples of two or more numbers

like terms   two or more terms that have exactly the same variable

line   a straight path that continues forever in two directions

line graph   graphic organizer that uses lines to display information that continues

major arc   an arc greater than or equal to 180 degrees

mean   the average of a set of data

median   the middle value in a set of numbers that are arranged in increasing or decreasing order. If there are two middle numbers, it is the average of these two.

midpoint   the point at the exact middle of a line segment

minor arc   an arc less than or equal to 180 degrees

mixed number   a number with an integer part and a fractional part. Mixed numbers can be converted into improper fractions.

mode   the value in a set of numbers that occurs most often. There can be one mode, several modes, or no mode.

multiple of   A number is a multiple of a second number if that second number can be multiplied by an integer to get the original number. *Example:* 10 is a multiple of 5 ($10 = 5 \times 2$); however, 10 is not a multiple of 3.

negative number   a number that is less than zero, such as –1, –18.6, –14.

numerator   the top part of a fraction. *Example:* 1 is the numerator in $\frac{1}{2}$.

obtuse angle   an angle that measures greater than 90 degrees

obtuse triangle   a triangle with an angle that measures greater than 90 degrees

odd integer   integers that aren't divisible by 2, such as –5, –3, –1, 1, 3, and so on

order of operations   the order in which operations are performed

ordered pair   a location of a point on a coordinate plane in the form (x,y).

origin   coordinate pair (0,0) and the point where the x- and y-axes intersect

parallel lines   two lines that do not intersect

percent   a ratio that compares numerical data to one hundred. The symbol for percent is %.

perimeter   the measure around a figure

perpendicular lines   lines that intersect to form right angles

pictograph   graphic organizer that uses pictures to represent a quantity

pie chart   circle graph that represents a whole, or 100%

positive number   a number that is greater than zero, such as 2, 42, $\frac{1}{2}$, 4.63

prime factorization   the process of breaking down factors into prime numbers

prime number   an integer that is divisible only by 1 and itself, such as 2, 3, 5, 7, 11, and so on. All prime numbers are odd, except for 2. The number 1 is not considered prime.

probability   the likelihood that a specific event will occur

product   the answer of a multiplication problem

proper fraction   a fraction whose numerator is less than its denominator

proportion   an equation that states that two ratios are equal

Pythagorean theorem   the formula $a^2 + b^2 = c^2$, where a and b represent the lengths of the legs and c represents the length of the hypotenuse of a right triangle

Pythagorean triple   a set of three integers that satisfies the Pythagorean theorem, such as 3:4:5

quadrilateral   a two-dimensional shape with four sides

quotient   the answer you get when you divide. *Example:* 10 divided by 5 is 2; the quotient is 2.

radical   the symbol used to signify a root operation

radicand   the number inside a radical

radius   the line segment whose one endpoint is at the center of the circle and whose other endpoint is on the circle

range   a number that indicates how close together the values are to each other in a set of data

ratio   a comparison of two things using numbers

ray   part of a line that has one endpoint and continues forever in one direction

reciprocal   the multiplicative inverse of a fraction. For example, $\frac{2}{1}$ is the reciprocal of $\frac{1}{2}$.

rectangle   a parallelogram with four right angles

remainder   The number left over after division. *Example:* 11 divided by 2 is 5, with a remainder of 1.

rhombus   a parallelogram with four equal sides

right angle   an angle that measures exactly 90 degrees

right triangle   a triangle with an angle that measures exactly 90 degrees

scalene triangle   a triangle with no equal sides

scatter plot   graphic organizer that uses horizontal and vertical axes to plot data points

simplify   to combine like terms and reduce an equation to its most basic form

slope   the steepness of a line

square   a parallelogram with four equal sides and four right angles

square of a number   the product of a number and itself, such as 4^2, which is 4×4

stem-and-leaf plot graphic organizer that splits the number data into a "stem" and a "leaf"

sum The sum of two numbers means the two numbers are added together.

supplementary angles two angles whose sum is 180 degrees

surface area the sum of the areas of the faces of a three-dimensional figure

table graphic organizer that arranges information into columns and rows

term a number, or a number and the variables associated with it

triangle a polygon with three sides

variables letters used to stand in for numbers

vertex a point at which two lines, line segments, or rays connect

vertical angles two opposite congruent angles formed by intersecting lines

volume a cubic measurement that measures how many cubic units it takes to fill a solid figure

NOTES

NOTES